State by State

WITH THE STATE

An Uninformed, Poorly Researched
Guide to the United States

by The State:

KEVIN ALLISON

MICHAEL IAN BLACK

BEN GARANT

MICHAEL PATRICK JANN

KERRI KENNEY

THOMAS LENNON

KEN MARINO

MICHAEL SHOWALTER

JOE LO TRUGLIO

DAVID WAIN

HYPERION

NEW YORK

HAPPY BIRTHDAY TO YOU, words and music by Mildred J. Hill and Patty S. Hill
© 1935 (Renewed) Summy-Birchard Music
All rights reserved   Made in USA
Used by Permission of WARNER BROS. PUBLICATIONS, INC., Miami, Fl. 33014

All art by The State with the exception of bottom photo on page 43, which is by
Cindy DiPrima.

Library of Congress Cataloging-in-Publication Data
State (Comedy group)
     State by state with the State : an uninformed, poorly researched guide to the
United States / State.—1st ed.
          p. cm.
     Includes index.
     ISBN 0-7868-8213-1
     1. United States—Description and travel—Humor. I. Title.
PN6231.T7S73 1997
917.304′929′0207—dc21 96–46335
CIP

Designed by Jessica Shatan

FIRST EDITION

10 9 8 7 6 5 4 3 2 1

To my husband, Ron:
My lover, my co-conspirator, and fellow chocoholic,
without whose support and patience
this would not have been possible.

This book is done, honey—you can have your bird room back!

We gratefully acknowledge the valuable contribution of Mollie Doyle for understanding, representing, enhancing our work; Cindy DiPrima for bringing visual life to our text; Carlo DiPalma for bringing visual life to many Woody Allen films.

Special thanks also to Brian DeFiore, Dan Strone, Steven Starr, James Dixon, Jon Bendis, and Jed Alpert.

CONTENTS

Chapter Eight: The Upper Left-Hand Corner 231

Chapter Nine: Alaska and Hawaii 243

Chapter Ten: Road Games 251

State by State

WITH THE STATE

Dear Reader,

A few years back, the members of the rock-and-roll band Judas Priest were accused of concealing satanic messages in its rock-and-roll recordings, a practice that we find unconscionable and inexcusable. For your convenience, following is an index to help you quickly locate the hidden satanic messages contained in this book.

Satanic Messages

p.57

p.108

p.164

Your friends,
The State

INTRODUCTION

O *beautiful for spacious skies, for amber waves of grain."*
We heard someone saying that phrase in reference to America last
year and it got us thinking, "Is it true or not?" Inspired and curious,
we set out on a mission to do something that to our knowledge is an
unprecedented first in publishing: a guidebook for traveling the
United States.

In order to truly document this great country, we needed to travel
the highways and byways, visiting every single state to see the spacious skies and amber waves up close. The ten of us quit our jobs as
the resident sketch comedy troupe on a cable music video channel,
packed our bags, piled in the orange van, and hit the open road.

What follows are the fruits of our journey: reports from places big
and small, travel tips, essays, stories, photographs, cartoons, journal
entries, road games, reviews, and the like.

So curl up on the couch and join The State, as we take you on our
American adventure: STATE BY STATE.

PACKING DOS AND DON'TS

Any trip in the United States is worth packing for. So don't be left
without Annette. (Total pun. Relax.)

If you're traveling by air, DO always use CARRY-ON luggage.
Small Girls should look for waterproof nylon with a high-density
weave. The Horny Young Man should bring a blanket when traveling by plane because when he needs to masturbate, the blanket provides coverage, shelter, and warmth for the hard penis.

What to Bring?

Please, for the sake of PHYLLIS DILLER, DO travel light! Kitties, shells, bean bread, and Tang are the only essentials. We like to call them "Must Brings." That's nothing more than a name we came up with. You can call them "must brings," too. Or if you prefer you can call them "gotta brings," "hafta brings," or "lefty hovis."

Clothing

Jeans! Jeans! Jeans! Eli Levi built canvas pants for the gold miners way back when. Now blue jeans are available in every major American city. DON'T hesitate to bring jeans—they are a welcome and comfortable pant for almost any travel situation. One reader told us someone even wore jeans in the WHITE HOUSE (?!?).

We've all had the embarrassing situation of unpacking a bag only to find a hopelessly wrinkled garment (*see* Phyllis Diller). Here's a tip: Wrinkles are easily remedied by removing them.

Here's a sample CLOTHING LIST:

2 prs. jeans (Levi's are good)

1 pr. shorts (again, Levi's)

4 denim work shirts (We hate to sound like a broken record or—worse—a spokesman for the Levi's people, but Levi's happens to make a good work shirt.)

1 jacket (We're not even gonna say it because we feel like we're going to get hit, but—okay, no. we're not gonna say it.)

DO please wear COMFORTABLE SHOES. If we had a nickel for every former member of Kiss (e.g., Bruce Kulik, Eric Singer) who came back sore from a day of city exploring having worn dragon boots with eight-inch heels, we'd be rich.

Toiletries and Accessories

A lot of travelers tend to forget that toiletries are things like shampoo and toothpaste, and not toilets. Commit this classic playground jump-rope rhyme to memory and the problem should evaporate:

> *Sir toothbrush, Miss shave cream and face washing rag,*
> *Toiletries are friends, they chill in your bag.*
> *As for Sir Toilet, he will not fit in it—*
> *He stays in your bathroom, his bowl's there to shit in it.*

Sample Packing List

Moneybelt/Pouch
Shortwave Radio (only necessary in remote areas)
Plastic Bags and a Few Ziploc Bags (not always needed)
Swiss Army Knife (only joking—you won't need one)
Earplugs (kidding)
Eyeshades (not)
Inflatable Pillow (wrong)
Travel Alarm Clock (I don't think so!)
Camera (as if)
Film (uh-uh)
Moist Towelettes (yeah, right?!)
Cards or Miniature Games (gimme a break)
Shoe Pouches (gimme a STEAK)
Guidebook(s) (I wouldn't mind a STEAK BREAK)
Book(s) for Pleasure Reading (that's a BREAK I could TAKE)
First-Aid Kit (Over at Pine Ridge LAKE)
Sarong (Do you like Vanilla Wafers?)
Tote Sack (I do)
Fanny Pack/Day Pack (knickknack paddywack)
Travel Umbrella (dip-dop dumbrella)
Travel Raincoat (seriously?)
Toiletry Bag (I wanna dip my BALLS in it!)
Small Locks for Luggage (Chicken SANDWICH, Carl!)

CHAPTER ONE

New England

Sometimes hailed as the "most boring part of the country,"

New England is actually a lot of fun—IF YOU KNOW WHERE TO LOOK! Unfortunately, we did not, and so we have to concur with the prevailing opinion about this scrubby American region.

Part of the problem with New England is the cold. If you go there during the winter, forget about it. It's really cold, and the only thing to do is sit around the fireplace and talk. Who wants to talk? During the summer, it's better, but unless you're really interested in commercial fishing, good luck finding stuff to do with yourself. The only fun thing to do in all of New England is to go to the *Cheers* bar in Boston. That's really fun because it looks like the bar on the TV show. One thing to do is to go there with a bunch of friends. Leave one friend outside, preferably a fat one, and then when he comes in, yell "Norm!" just like on the TV show.

Some people think we should give New England to the Canadians in exchange for their half of Niagara Falls. We agree. Wouldn't it be worth unloading some of our lesser states in exchange for all the cool stuff on the Canadian side of the Falls (wax museums, strip clubs, and video games that take Canadian "money")? If that doesn't convince you, think about this: If we gave Vermont to Canada, you would actually save money skiing there because the Canadian dollar is worth less than the American! Of course, we may have to pay slightly more for pure maple syrup, but who cares? Pure maple syrup is kind of stupid, anyway.

There are some redeeming things about New England: the Manhattan clam chowder, for one. Also, the summer stock theater, which is consistently good. No place in the nation boasts as many oil paintings of ships at sea as New England. But the pizza sucks, and there's almost no gangsta rap.

MAINE

MAINE

Maine Factoid

Up in Bangor, Maine, you're allowed to run around town yelling "Bangor? Bangor? I wish. I only got a hand job!!!" until 9 P.M. EST.

A Bit of History about . . . Mane?

As we all know, the United States looks not unlike a poodle with a few glorious birth defects:

Poodle

The United States

Native American legend says that our country was modeled after God's poodle, whose name was James Cambell-Holland. Scientific Research and the Abenaki Indian folklore seem to agree on the point of the existence of such a poodle, but science seems to suggest that the dog's name was Jonas Spenser. Furthermore, it seems that the insane notion that this dog had birth defects was nothing more than a misinterpretation by the mostly stupid Native American population. What they were referring to was simply a major disfigurement the dog had suffered from being shoved into a mailing tube a few minutes AFTER birth.

And such is the reason why our American poodle has such a small head.

And yet, God started calling the head of the beast MAINE, as if

 Travelers' Advisory

Small-Town Murders

Sure, small-town murders seem quaintly intriguing in "movies" and on "TV," and yes, we all loved Sidney Poitier's portrayal of Mr. Tibbs and indeed Angela Lansbury made it look easy every Sunday night, but in real life, small-town murders are **NO LAUGHING MATTER.** If there's one sure-fire way to ruin your vacation, it's by getting involved in a small-town murder investigation. Don't be an asshole. If you find a dead body somewhere while you're on vacation, **DON'T DO ANYTHING.** Don't call the police, and for damn sure **DON'T TOUCH IT.** Get in the car and drive. Take your amateur sleuthing pipe dreams and stick 'em up your ass. Remember: You don't have an alibi and "TV" and "movies" are bullshit. Just drive the car and pray to God that the body rots beyond recognition before anybody ever finds it.

the head of the poodle were as large as a lion's mane! As brutally ironic as it was, the nickname stuck. (For other stuck nicknames, see "Babe" Ruth, "Fritz" Mondale, and Theodore "Ted" Turner.)

Maine**Destinations**

Mount Desert Island

The Down East/Acadia region of Maine is only a 475-mile drive from New York City. (When in New York, check out the exciting Broadway shows. While *Cats* and *Les Miserables* are old standbys, why not try something daring and certifiably offbeat like *Phantom*?)

Mount Desert Island was discovered by a Frenchman—Samuel de Champlain, who named it Ile des Monts, which means "Island of Bare Mountains" (*see* Dollywood, Tennessee). The first settlers were French, which explains why nearly every McDonald's in the region sells "French Fries." When the French were defeated in Canada,* the British settled here. The British influence can be seen in the way that most of the locals are kind of annoying, just the same way most if not all British people are.

Bar Harbor

Think lobster. Think deep-sea fishing. Think eclectic boutiques. Now you're in the Bar Harbor groove.

Search the world—only Jerusalem sells more fresh lobster than Bar Harbor, Maine.

No-frills dining in Maine.

The thing to do in Bar Harbor is to stop in at one of these seaside dives—and no kidding, these places are NO FRILLS. And you pick a lobster, they boil it up, and you

---

*Canada is outside the scope of this book. Please consult one of the many fine travel publications by the Kids in the Hall.

literally sit on a wooden bench and eat the damn thing. Just don't try this with vegetarian friends, because every time you crack the thing open, they'll groan, "Ahhh—you just broke another bone, you barbarian!" (Suggested comeback: "Lobsters have an exoskeleton—it's ALL bone, you fucker!")

highway tip

STATE TROOPERS

If you're like us, you get pulled over by the county mounties practically every damn time you're coked up and behind the wheel. Here's a little tip for all our fellow scofflaws that's sure to get you off the hook and back on the road lickety-split. The next time a Smokey asks to see your driver's license, follow these simple steps:

1. Explain to the officer that you might have left your driver's license "under your balls."
2. Slowly reach down, unzip your fly, and gingerly extract your balls.
3. Wiggle your balls around a little, give 'em a good show.
4. Sit back and let Johnny Law drink in the eye candy.
5. Kiss your worries good-bye. There's nothing the pigs love like a little Testes Fiesta. You might want to keep a stack of Polaroid shots of your balls in the glove compartment to leave them with a little memento.

NEW HAMPSHIRE

NEW HAMPSHIRE

STATE IT LOOKS LIKE AN UPSIDE-DOWN VERSION OF:
Vermont

STATES IT DOESN'T LOOK LIKE AN UPSIDE-DOWN VERSION
OF: Hawaii, Michigan, and Florida

HIGHEST POINT: Mt. Washington

LOWEST POINT: Mt. Reagan/Bush

FAVORITE JACKSON: (tie) Kate, Jesse and Action

DIRECTOR OF PHOTOGRAPHY: Gordon Willis, A.S.C.

How to Get There by Car
The long thin thing (shaped like Bert) makes it go, and the wider, shorter pedal (shaped like Ernie) makes it stop.

State Law You Should Know About
Any grainy black-and-white pictures taken of homeless people will be confiscated and the photographer will be given a three-year sentence in a maximum security prison.

Interesting Facts about New Hampshire

New Hampshire was first settled in 1623, by fur, fish, and timber merchants. Most if not all of the original settlers have since passed away. Their families request that instead of flowers, donations in memory of these merchants be sent to the Ronald McDonald House.

Today's New Hampshire is more than just mountains, forests, and streams. Travelers in this modern state will also find ponds, hills, and lakes. And while it's no Skokie, there are Jews there.

New Hampshire**Events**

The New Hampshire Venereal Disease Festival

If you're like us, you've had your share of venereal diseases. So, we had to check this out. Some of the highlights were:

The VD Tee Pee Here you can sit in an authentic wigwam with several locals dressed as Indians and reminisce about sexually transmitted diseases with the spirits.

The Crab Walk Walk through acres of crab-infested pubic thicket . . . but watch where you step!!

The Clap Shack Great burgers!

General Genital Wart The mascot of the festival. Bring your camera, he's double jointed!

The Chlamydiots A half-hour fun-filled variety show, with singing, dancing, and more chlamydia than you can shake a stick at. A cross between the Keystone Kops and chlamydia.

New Hampshire**Nightlife**

If you're in New Hampshire and looking for a really good rhythm-and-blues bar, get on Route 99, turn south, and then keep driving until you hit a state that's not all white people.

FROM JOE'S SKETCHBOOK —

New Hampshire's BRADS!

BRAD KESSNER
BOYFRIEND

BRAD PAOLILLO
CROSSING GUARD

BRAD DALY
ASSISTANT MANAGER

BRAD GUSHUE
PROJECTIONIST

BRAD SINOPOLI
PHOTO LAB TECHNICIAN

From Showalter's Journal

sunset, Lake Winnepasakee
I noticed that in New Hampshire certain
phrases are really popular, like, "Open
the fridge, Mom! I gots ta poop!," "Dang!
My vagina is, like, totally bustin' outta
my britches!," "I'm full of that damn
poop and it sucks! Poop sucks, Dude!,"
and my personal favorite, "Wieners.
Wieners and VJs. Wieners and VJs rule!"
Not to mention, "Poop's everywhere, man!
Gotta get that the hell outta here!" and,
of course, "Vagina! What the hell???"

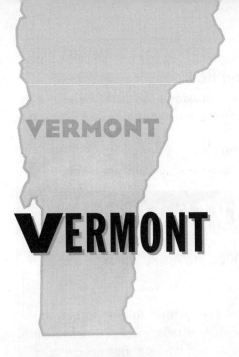

VERMONT

VERMONT

Vermont Factoid
Wearing shorts in Vermont is considered "showing off."

State Law You Should Know About
Any Vermont actor who uses "Jazz Hands" in a performance or audition is fined a minimum of $1,000.

A Bit of History from Vermont
The first and last "Slide Naked and Face First Down Stowe Mountain Race" was held March 8, 1898.

Vermont**Attractions**

Robert Frost's Old Boots
Imagine Robert Frost in his old boots . . . sends shivers down the spine.

Robert Frost's Big Chair
Sit in Robert Frost's big chair. Imagine what it must have been like for him to sit in it.

Robert Frost's Fishing Rod

Touch Robert Frost's fishing rod. Imagine a fish on the end of that rod and then imagine that Robert Frost was the one holding the fishing rod.

Robert Frost's Hammock

Lie down in Robert Frost's hammock . . . um . . . take a nap.

TRAVEL TIP

Recommended Travel Products

AIR TRAVEL DARTS ($18.95)
This handsome dart set comes with a folding target and leather case that can be stowed neatly under the seat in front of you during takeoff and landing. But once you're in the air, the fun begins! Simply hang the target on a seat five rows away and enjoy a sky-high game of darts. (Recommended for intermediate and advanced dart players only.)

LIZARD MILK ($3/GALLON)
The most common question we're asked: "I'm traveling with children, and they always want to feed lizards on the road. What do I tell them?" Fret no more, because as the famous commercial says, "Lizards love Lizard Milk." (Available in Chocolate, Tuna, and Bologna.)

BERTINELLI'S CITATION BUSTER SERVICE ($300)
Next time you get pulled over for speeding, you'll go free with this valuable service. When you see the cop's flashers, you call a special 800 number on your car phone. Just stall the cop until One Day at a Time's Valerie Bertinelli shows up and sweet-talks your way to freedom. (Car phone not included.)

MASSACHUSETTS

Massachusetts Factoid
Slavery is still legal.

A Bit of History from Massachusetts
In 1877, Puritan minister Loy Merch of Larchmont, Massachusetts, develops the first known CD-ROM technology.

In the state of Massachusetts, any spinster (unmarried woman over the age of 21) must register at a notary public and receive a Boatswain's Lanyard, which she may remove on the Sabbath and during Lent.

State Law You Should Know About
Saying you don't watch TV, if you do, is considered the same as first-degree manslaughter in Massachusetts.

MassachusettsAttractions

The Natural Cat Geyser of Wooster, Massachusetts

There is only one completely natural cat geyser in the United States, and it is at Prowkey Park in the heart of Wooster. Every day at 4:17, hundreds of elderly and grotesquely overweight cats bubble up out of Brunswick Crevice. Unfortunately, most of the cats surface dead, and nearly all of them are HIV positive, making Prowkey Park the most dangerous tourist attraction in the world. Rumor has it that the National Guard is going to shut it down this year, so get there before it's too late!

THINGS TO DO IF YOU'RE BORED IN MASSACHUSETTS

1. Check out the "Punch A Euro Guy In The Face For Free" stand, in Cambridge.
2. For men, visit the Museum of Gorgeous Breasts and Stomachs; and for the ladies, visit the Museum of Guys Who Can Make You Laugh and Listen Well.
3. Go to "Pappy's Bar" on Main Street and listen to Vietnam veterans talk about Saigon, napalm, and Santana.
4. Stop in at K-mart and see how many candy bars you can steal.
5. Pretend it's the late 1700s and start a war.

The Massachusetts Glass Museum, Flume, Massachusetts

Just off of Highway 32, north of Gilbertville, the Massachusetts Glass Museum is much more interesting than it sounds. The subject matter of its exhibits is not even, in fact, glass.

The museum instead contains one of the most extensive collections of French, English, and German thrones in the world—some of them dating back as far as the third century A.D.

It's the museum itself that's made of glass—a converted manor once owned by a wealthy industrialist and spun entirely of glass and crystal by New England's finest craftsmen.

The museum is currently under extensive repairs, however, and will not be reopened until the fall of '99, due to its complete collapse.

I guess it goes to show you. People in glass houses shouldn't stow thrones. Thank you, folks. Thank you very much. I love you all. Good night, folks.

The Ennui Biscuit Contest, Rutherford, Massachusetts

People from all over bring in their homemade biscuits which they feel emote a certain sense of ennui. The biscuits are put on a long table and everyone in town looks them over for hours and hours. Then they vote. The biscuit filled with the most ennui is crowned and placed on a counter. To be honest with you, I really couldn't tell the biscuits apart.

The United States: What's in a Name?

How did the United States get such a kooky name? No one knows for sure. Early historians used to think that it referred to the fact that all the states were united under one federal government! (?!?)

Most likely, our country is named after two groups of people: a group of Massachusetts settlers called The United (1754–1819); and a group of New York comedians called The State (1988–1996). Rigorous carbon dating is under way right now, and proof of this should arrive within weeks. The expected proof might be photographs and sworn testimony to the effect that, yes, the scientists are performing the carbon dating.

And for those of you who are fans of <u>Mad</u> magazine style humor, here's one for you: America got its name from the Italian explorer Amerigo Vespuke-all-over-me.

Restaurant Round-Up

Great Dishes at Restaurants in Nantucket and Martha's Vineyard

★ ★ ★ ★ ★ ★ ★ ★ ★ ★ ★ ★ ★ ★ ★ ★

PJ's Hamburger-Sized Clambellies *PJ's Hamburger Sized Clam Restaurant, Martha's Vineyard.* If you love seafood, then you'll go belly up for these clams. They're huge. They're the size of hamburgers.

Mostly Corn *The Grismer Inn, Martha's Vineyard.* This dish has an odd but memorable flavor, and it seems like it's mostly corn.

Aspirin Cake *Lakeshore Steakhouse, Martha's Vineyard.* Deeeelish!

Supposed to be Porridge *Murphy's, Nantucket.* It's suppose to be porridge, but it's actually chicken salad. Who cares? It tastes great!

Lead Sammy's *Lead Sammy's, Nantucket.* Short for lead sandwiches, lead sammy's are just that—sandwiches made with lead. The fixin's make it truly special.

Doggy Soup *The Red Rose, Nantucket.* It's probably not really dog in the soup, but even if it is . . . goddammit that shit is goood!

★ ★ ★ ★ ★ ★ ★ ★ ★ ★ ★ ★ ★ ★ ★ ★

RHODE ISLAND

STATE TEETH: The Bicuspids

MIDGET POPULATION: 78 percent

MOST POPULAR CHARADES GESTURE:
"Sounds like"

CONNECTION TO THE KENNEDY ASSASSINATION:
Some

STATE DRINK: Dirty White Mother

GOOD-LOOKING ASIAN BOYS: 326

MOST POPULAR HEPATITIS STRAIN: B

Interesting Fact about Rhode Island

Rhode Island is the only state that is entirely carpeted. The job required 846 square miles of stain-resistant carpet and cost $38,000. Padding and installation were included. It's a sort of reddish-brown medium shag. It's nice.

Red Flag Hitchhikers

Rhode Island

"MILK"

Travelers' Advisory

Assassination Cyborgs

The road is a great place to make friends—and the drifters and teenage runaways that roam our nation's highways set the international standard for drifters and teenage runaways. Yet be advised: Assassination Cyborgs should be avoided at all costs. Take this helpful quiz and prevent yourself from being exterminated by one of the twenty-first-century's supersoldiers.

Question 1: Is your new friend's skin exceedingly cold to the touch?

Question 2: Do his/her pupils dilate in the presence of a microwave oven?

Question 3: Can your new friend run, shoot, and kill with superhuman ability?

If you answered yes to any of these questions, get away before you die in any of a thousand ways.

Driving toward Rhode Island this afternoon, we passed a sign that read "Livermore Junior College. Next Exit." Well, that sign was enough to start Black thinking about his time in junior college and about a guy he knew way back then. . . .

PAT
Who Was Hell with His Fists

When I was in junior college I knew a guy named Pat who was hell with his fists. Everybody thought Pat was the tops, but nobody messed with him. Nobody would dare, because Pat was hell with his fists.

One day, there was a mean guy who started calling Pat names for no reason at all, and it seemed to all of us watching that this mean guy was itching for a fight. But Pat didn't want to fight, so he just kept walking. The mean guy was calling Pat terrible names. Names like "Chicken" and "Fraidy Cat!" Pat kept walking though and didn't pay that mean guy no mind. Then the mean guy started calling Pat's girlfriend names, and Pat was steamed!!! But he didn't punch the guy because Pat was reading a book about Gandhi.

But then the mean guy started calling Pat's mother names, and that was too much even for Pat. Everybody knew Pat's mother was a saint who had died saving a hat from a burning building. Pat stopped right in his tracks, and when that happened we all knew Pat was finally going to use those fabled fists of his, because Gandhi is one thing, but a guy's mother, by definition, is something else entirely. Many people said, "Don't do it, Pat," and "No, Pat," but Pat couldn't hear those people. He was lost in a world of his own, a world not unlike our own planet Earth, but without all those people who were telling Pat not to punch the mean guy.

Pat's eyes grew very big, and his hands curled up into tight little balls, or to put it another, more succinct, way, fists. Then Pat reared back his mighty hands and punched the mean guy as hard as he could, even though by now the whole crowd was screaming, "No, Pat!"

Well, what do you think happened then? We all heard a terrible sound, a sound we all recognized from movies in which bones broke. It was the sound of bones breaking, and then we saw a man on the ground in terrible pain. And who do you think that man was? It was Pat! Pat, who was hell with his fists! He was lying in the road holding his broken fists and saying certain swear words like "Damn!" and "Damn It!"

You see, Pat had discovered what the rest of the crowd had been warning him about when they had said, "Don't do it, Pat," and "No, Pat!" They had noticed something that Pat, in his anger, couldn't see. They had noticed that the mean guy was made out of CONCRETE! He was a concrete man, the only one any of us had ever seen, and what's more, he was a transfer student.

The mean guy just stood there laughing, and after a while some of the people in the crowd began laughing, too. Pretty soon, everybody was laughing, because even though we all felt bad for Pat, it was kind of funny that he had tried to punch a guy made out of concrete. Pat walked away alone, and the mean guy took us all out for fries. It turns out his name was Steve, and he wasn't so mean after all.

I lost touch with Pat after that. We all did. He dropped out of school and died a few years later from a stomach disease that he left untreated because he was reading a book about Christian Scientists.

TRAVEL TIP

How to Use Maps

"The toe bone's connected to the foot bone . . ."
                              —traditional American folk song

Connections. What is the world without them? One need look no further than the classic baby carriage sequence in Eisenstein's seminal work <u>Potemkin</u>. And maps are quite literally the road maps on our journey across the nation.

A couple of misconceptions about maps that we've heard on our travels:

1. "Maps are the same size as the area of land they represent." Not true. On balance, maps tend to be much, much smaller.

2. "If I have the right maps, gasoline is free." The reality is that gas costs the same whether or not you have the right maps.

3. "If the map shows a road that leads south, chances are that if I follow it, I'll end up in a nudist camp and within minutes be making love to a foxy nude lady who resembles Cheryl Ladd." Ha! We had to laugh when we heard this one. Cheryl Ladd! Try Priscilla Barnes. That's more like it. The babe'll look quite a bit more like Priscilla Barnes.

CONNECTICUT

CONNECTICUT

Nuthin'

CHAPTER TWO

The North Atlantic Coastal States

The most densely populated area of the United States,

this region of the Northeast is home to more people than the tiny island nations of Fiji and Togo combined! In fact, literally hundreds of people call the North Atlantic Coastal States home, and for good reason—they live there.

First settled in 1912 by roller-coaster enthusiasts, the Northeast quickly became home to some of the nation's premier roller coasters: "The Cyclone," "The Screaming Machine," and the unfortunately named "Grandma's Saggy Boob," which opened and closed in 1936.

Geographically, the North Atlantic Coastal States are comprised primarily of water and dirt. Some of the water is salty and some is fresh, but all of it follows the classic chemical equation H_2O. The dirt tends to be crumbly, with some of it moist and suitable for farming, and some of it different from that.

Fans of Frank Sinatra will be interested to know that Ol' Blue Eyes was born in the Northeast, as were many famous people, including the present Queen of England, still known in her hometown of Passaic, New Jersey, as simply "Queeny."

While there is no unifying cultural characteristic of "The Northeasterner," our research supports the finding that most of the region's inhabitants fall into several categories: they tend either to have deeply held religious convictions or not; they tend to spend American money at more than double the rate they spend South African money; as a group they tend to vote for either the Democratic or Republican parties if they vote at all; they prefer their personal mail to be delivered to their homes and their business mail to their offices; they sometimes jokingly refer to their spouses as "my better half"; most rate Mickey Mouse as "friendly" or "very friendly"; and nearly all of them feel some measure of respect for George Foreman, the boxer.

If you keep these things in mind when visiting the North Atlantic Coastal States, it's practically guaranteed that not only will you have a good time, you will win a great deal of money and fall in love with your lifelong soul mate.

NEW YORK

NEW YORK

UpstateNY**Destinations**

Niagara Falls
Just like the pictures, but bigger. Also noisier.

NewYorkCity**Guide**

Museums in Review
The assholes who run the stupid Metropolitan Museum of "Art" are a bunch of uptight, elitist assholes. They will not let you in without a shirt, no matter how badly you need to use the can.

I say, "Suck me, Metropolitan Museum!" And your stupid "Art."

Entering New York City
If the Holland Tunnel should crack open while you're driving through it, just before you're killed by millions of gallons of the Hudson River, the radio reception, for a moment, will be perfect.

There are also some bridges into New York, but they're closed for the filming of *Die Hard 4*.

Little Italy

If you're in scenic Little Italy and you want more of an adventure than just the basic dinner, cannoli, and cappuccino, then try this: Put on a velveteen sweat suit, a fake mustache, and large sunglasses; walk into any store, restaurant, or bakery; and proudly say, "I'm the man who brought down the Genovese Crime Family!"

Gingerbread Alley

One block south of Delancey on the old Bowery, Gingerbread Alley isn't quite the spectacle that it was in its heyday, a time when Edna St. Vincent Millay described it as ". . . equal parts heaven and pastry." Gingerbread, as a material, does not weather well, and after almost two centuries of wear and tear most of the once quaint cottages are dilapidated and moist. The gingerbread men that still

The unmistakable NYC skyline.

parade the alley every hour on the half hour have taken on the bedraggled look of a band of lepers. Don't try to bite them, as their rotten, wormy, gingerflesh carries a horrible strain of salmonella—and these days, the doped-up gingerbread men are likely to bite back. It's best to wrap up your visit before sundown, when packs of rats descend on the alley and the air fills with the howls of little baked men as they are devoured alive.

Mike Jann's Apartment, Lower East Side

Not to be missed when in New York! This shabby, overpriced hovel is home to unemployed filmmaker Mike Jann, who, though unable to make any kind of living off his trade, has been assured by his agent that good things are just around the corner. Weekends often find Mike in his living room/kitchen smoking pot and forcing his friends to watch obscure Asian films with no subtitles. Visitors are encouraged to bring LOTS of cigarettes, as Mr. Jann, who smokes two packs a day, refuses to buy his own. First-timers will immediately notice the unpretentious decor. Curling pages torn from previously owned French design magazines mingle harmoniously on walls full of "Great Movie Idea" notecards and vague Hindu icons. His luxurious brown sofa sits in stark contrast to his not-so-luxurious brown sleeping bag. But the real attraction here is the man himself. A study in contradictions, Mr. Jann eagerly holds lengthy court on topics ranging from "Texture and Tonality in the Early Works of Bresson and Kitano" to "Why I'm a Bad Person and Deserve to Be Poor," all while sucking down whippets and Pernod. A lucky few may be invited to hear how he predicted the emergence of "Grunge" as a mainstream phenomenon months before the fact. Even the heartiest of thrill-seekers will wish to avoid the topic of Catholicism. Visitors are encouraged to shut-the-fuck-up and listen. *(Cash or barter. No credit.)*

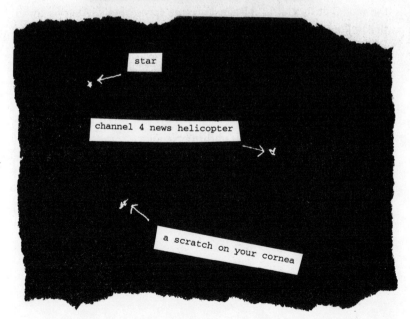

SoHo

On exiting this fabulous New York attraction, the general tourist reaction can be summed up as, "Jesus, I feel fat." Formerly a hip, downtown mix of painters, musicians, and kooky performance artists, the entire area was demolished during the stock market boom in 1983 and rebuilt as a wildlife sanctuary for fashion models. SoHo is an excellent environment for viewing these rarefied creatures in their natural habitat. Watch the models forage for tiny bottles of Italian soft drinks. Be amazed when they use their natural camouflage to blend seamlessly into a newsstand full of fashion magazines. Marvel at the splendor of these perfectly proportioned animals as they hunt down and brutally slaughter younger models! But don't get too close to the creatures. The deep tranquil elegance of their disdainful stares has been known to kill those with a poor self-image. Also, the fragile ecosystem is delicately balanced. Those visitors not able to make a living off their physical beauty will be asked to leave. "It's for the protection of the tourists," says Park Ranger/Fashion Photographer Helmut Gutling. "I once saw a very fat child ripped limb from limb. It was horrible. We had to send all the models to a spa in Alsace-Lorraine for a week." Also be aware that the awesome natural power of the animals' credit limits makes shopping a no-no. Content yourself instead with a window seat at a local cafe, and enjoy a $5 cup of Cafe Americain (French for crappy truck-stop coffee).

Page 40 S'up Check

Dude; S'up? S'up dude? You chillin? S'cool.

How you diggin' page 40? (Wasn't page 24 way fucked up?) Yeah, well. Take it easy, dude. Keep on Keepin' on. Am I right? Am I right? I love you, dude?

NEW JERSEY

Visiting the "Fourteenth Colony"

Almost all Americans remember the original thirteen colonies from their school days. And until recently, thirteen was America's "lucky number." But recent archeological and cosmetic advancements have discovered a lost fourteenth colony. Located directly across the Atlantic Ocean on a large island, this fourteenth colony, or "England," was home to millions of English-speaking settlers. Unlike the other thirteen colonies, however, England had castles, a Parliament, and, later, "the Fab Four." While some historians still question England's very existence, many more are debating the reasons why it was not represented on the original American flag and why English delegates were not sent to sign the Declaration of Independence. One theory is that because of its geographical isolation, England developed separately and became, in a sense, its own country. Some crackpots have even suggested that the white man colonized England thousands of years before the other thirteen colonies, a theory to which we reply, "Poppycock!"

Directions to the Fourteenth Colony

Drive east (you may have to take a ferry).

A CONVERSATION Overheard between two older women at the slot machines in the Trump Castle Casino in Atlantic City:

CLAIRE: Madeline, why don't you have a drink, the cocktail gal is coming this way.

MADELINE: Quit telling me what to do, Claire.

CLAIRE: I'm not telling you what to do, I'm just telling you the girl is coming this way. If you don't want something free that's up to you. I don't care what you do. *(To the waitress)* I'll have another one of these please . . . and my friend will have the same. *(CLAIRE's machine goes "ding ding ding." Coins start pouring out.)* See that? *(She yells right in Madeline's face.)* That's a winner, Madeline! That's a winner! *(The coins stop.)*

MADELINE: Good for you, Claire. I'm going up to the room. I'll see you at dinner.

CLAIRE: Where are you going?

MADELINE: I just said, I'm going up to the room. I'm tired of your "harazzing." *(Madeline leaves.)*

CLAIRE: *(To herself)* That's not even a word, "harazzing." *(Yelling off to Madeline)* "Harazzing" isn't a word, Madeline! *(To herself again)* That bitch. I never liked her. *(Yelling off to Madeline)* Wait up, Madeline, I'm coming with you! Wait up!

•*see the sights of*•
GLORIOUS NEW JERSEY

The Pagoda of the Six Harmonies

The Pagoda of the Six Harmonies is located in China, not New Jersey. This is a bad bit of luck for both the inhabitants of New Jersey and anyone passing through, as the area would be considerably more interesting were it home to the world-famous pagoda. If you've never seen this incredible pagoda, you have no idea what you're missing.

Tienanmen Square

Nowhere at all near New Jersey is the "Mother of All Squares." Over 120 acres in the center of Beijing, it has been the sight of countless historic demonstrations, all of which directly concerned the politics of China and certainly not New Jersey.

Hong Kong Island

If you're planning on spending any time on Hong Kong Island while in New Jersey you may want to take into consideration that it's twelve thousand miles away. Even with today's advanced transporta-

tion technology, to call this metropolis "convenient" to even the eastern-most parts of New Jersey would be a sad mistake. It is, after all, twelve hours to get there by plane from Heathrow Airport in London, which is itself quite a good distance from New Jersey.

Nanfang Department Store

Nanfang Department Store was where I met my friend Huong. Oh Huong. . . . Now how the poet's words resound in my reveries, ". . . he knew too well the sick, sick dread lest the one he lov'd might secretly be indifferent to him." I don't want to talk about it.

The Great Wall

What the fuck is wrong with you? Can you not understand that China is on the other fucking side of the planet? You're worse than

Huong. Listen, my aunt Betsy works with a lot of "special people." Can I just give you her number? It's 011-81-565-1212. Are you gonna call? Call already!

TOP SECRET PAGES

(only political exiles may read these pages)

If you are a "tourist" seeking refuge from an oppressive government regime, then follow these instructions for safe and thorough asylum here in America.

1. New York City's meatpacking district (Washington and 14th). You're looking for a pimp named Flash. Tell him you're "looking for some transvestite lovin'." This is the code phrase for "I need fake identification." If for any reason Flash responds by giving you a transvestite, tell him that there's been a misunderstanding and what you actually need is some fake identification.

2. Next stop, Washington, D.C., our nation's capital. The Air and Space Museum. Go to the Space Shuttle exhibit and look for a man wearing matching Yankees shirt and shorts. If he asks you, "Are you a die-hard Yankees fan?" then walk away. That man is an autistic millionaire's man/child named Livingston. He'll only waste your time. Keep looking for the other man in the matching Yankees shirt and shorts. Once you've found him he will know that you're a refugee seeking asylum if you say this to him, "I'm a refugee seeking asylum and I need your help." His name is "Bert Convy." He will provide you with names and places of people in the area who can provide you with a list of names and places of people in the area who can help.

3. Marin County, California. 116 La Playa Boulevard. You'll be meeting Veronica Merminclamp and her husband, Berb. Tell them you've just seen *La Traviata* for the tenth time and you can't wait to see it again. This should break the ice. They love opera. If that doesn't work, if things still seem a little awkward or uncomfortable, ask Berb how he likes his new PC. If after that point conversation doesn't pick up, then we suggest you leave and come back the next day and try the *La Traviata* line again. If conversation does pick up then, at a point in the conversation that seems appropriate to you, make subtle hints that you're interested in selling secrets about your government to the CIA. Veronica and Berb will find this very amusing. If they don't find it amusing then it's a

setup and you should run away as fast as you can. But if they do, then CONGRATULATIONS! You're well on your way to safe asylum.

4. If you're in a rush or just prefer a much easier way of dealing with this, then skip numbers 1, 2, and 3 and go to The C.F.F.S.A.F.R.O.O.G.R. (The Center for Finding Safe Asylum for Refugees of Oppressive Government Regimes). The Center is located in Dorchester, Massachusetts, on Oak Avenue across the street from Friendly's (the chocolate Fribble is to die for). There's a very nice man there who will help you with whatever you need. It's a very simple process apparently and of a very high priority to the U.S. government so, we've heard, that they'll take pretty good care of you.

(Aren't sure if your government is oppressive? For a list of oppressive government regimes check out our other books: *The State Gets Communal in Eastern Europe, The State's Wild African Safari,* and *Viva The State! Fun in Central America.*)

DELAWARE

A Bit of History from Delaware

In 1957, fourteen customers of JEFF'S HIGHWAY DINER all report to have seen Big Foot enter the restaurant and order a cup of coffee, two scrambled eggs, a cinnamon Danish, three bowls of cereal, a bagel with a schmear, five sides of bacon, an egg salad sandwich, nine blueberry pancakes, a blondie, and refill on the coffee.

Delaware Factoid

The Mayor of Wilmington, Delaware, Jerrod Scrins, is the only registered fascist in the United States. He has been the mayor of Wilmington since 1953, when he overthrew the incumbent mayor after losing a close election and declared himself mayor. In addition, he declared himself the Best Singer in Delaware and the World's Sexiest Man Alive.

State Law You Should Know About

If you haven't seen *Jaws*, you are held without bail and prosecuted to the full extent of the law. Conversely, if you give someone shit for not having seen a movie, you, too, are subject to hard time in jail.

Delaware?

No other state in the Union is as shrouded in mystery as that miniature jewel in the Eastern Seaboard's crown, the great state of
Delaware. When the topic of urbane dinner party conversation
invariably turns to Delaware, the same questions are on everyone's
lips, questions like, "Delaware? Isn't that where all the banks are?"
and "Delaware's a state? I thought it was a bank." Well, as most edu-
cated people know, Delaware is not a banking institution but a tax
shelter for DuPont Corporation. Sure, Delaware likes to claim to
actually be a full-fledged member of the United States of America.
While that is technically true, most Americans think of Delaware the
same way that *Price Is Right* contestants who've won a Cadillac and a
world cruise in the Showcase Showdown think of the ugly brown carpeting they won earlier in the program. We won the American
Revolution, we beat the British, and Delaware was just some carpet
that came as part of the package. The fact that our Founding Fathers
didn't chainsaw it off the continent and let it sink into the sea is a
testament to the good graces of the rest of the nation.

 Travelers' Advisory

If you're tired you might not notice, but Delaware is the only
state in America that doesn't have gravity. If you're traveling
through Delaware be sure to stop at your local K-mart and
pick up a pair of Uranium Lead Booties. Otherwise you'll float
up into the stratosphere and pop.

DelawareEvents

American Symphony Alcoholic Orchestra

World premiere of renowned Alcoholic Brian O'Neil's Slurring Loud
Run-On Sentences about Women Who Have "Screwed Us in the

Ass More Than Once." Leo McKinny conducts and pours from Stool. BYOB. Port-o-potties available.

The Annual One-Mile Sloatsworth Poodle Race, Sloatsworth, Delaware

fun fact

If you took every resident of Delaware and placed them one on top of another in a big pile that stretched up to the moon, a lot of them would probably die!

★

"If you haven't taken part in this thirty-seven-year Delaware tradition," says Fred Strevel of the Sloatsworth Chamber of Commerce, between long sensuous drags of his fine, imported cigarette, "then you haven't seen Delaware." He took another drag of his cigarette, crushed it out on the clean linoleum floor of his office, kissed Ben—for what would turn out to be the last bittersweet time—and walked out into the cold November rain. We would never see Fred Strevel again. In Delaware or anyplace.

The one-mile poodle race starts at 1 P.M. exactly, and the record time is held by James Eudworn and his poodle Katharine Hepburn. The winning time: .27 seconds.

Since the mid-sixties, the ASPCA has been trying to outlaw the use of artificial Poodle Starting Mechanisms, to no avail.

"They obviously don't understand the race," comments Mark Edworn. Mark and his poodle Lisa Marie are this year's favorites. Lisa Marie will be starting the race from a modified tennis ball launcher, outfitted with three washing machine engines, an outboard motor, and some sort of surplus G.E. turbine.

fun fact

Did you know that all four million residents of Delaware were chemically engineered?!

★

"It's the same design I used last year, but I think I got most of the bugs out," says Mark.

Along with the coveted Golden Piddles Trophy (named after the race's first winner), most winners are approached by Lockheed Aerodynamics with big money offers.

At 12:45 we took our seats as the poodles were dyed for easy identification at the finish line. Tension mounted. Then, at 1:00, the race was over, before the starting gun's smoke had even cleared.

And Lisa Marie not only won the race but broke all previous records with a time of .07 seconds.

Mark Edworn, however, was killed by an obvious flaw in the recoil design of his washing machines. One thing's for sure, we'll be back next year!

THE DELAWARE FUNNIES

It is the nature of any good traveler to arrive in a new town and be eager to learn its history, people, and traditions. Even though many of us had passed through Delaware, none of us had ever really actually stayed there before. So when we arrived we set out to discover what this state of little repute was all about. David had compiled a list of questions that could be asked of anyone, the answers to which would provide us with a good idea of what kind of folk we were dealing with. Question #5 was, "What's your favorite comic strip?" Overwhelmingly, the people of Delaware cited a strip in their local rag *The Delawarian* called "The Delaware Funnies." So we picked up a copy of our own, and here's what we found:

The sentiments expressed in the comic seemed a bit odd to us. We sensed some anti-Semitism in the piece that offended members of the group but chose to give the good people of Delaware, who loved this cartoon with almost fanatical enthusiasm, the benefit of the doubt. We waited a day and picked up another copy of *The Delawarian* fully expecting to have our misgivings put to rest. This is what we found:

Again the subtle anti-Semitism reared its head in the piece. When we asked people why they loved the cartoon so much the most common response was, ". . . because we hate Jews." This made us uncomfortable but we were determined to look deeper. The next day we picked up another copy of the paper and the results were less than encouraging. We read *The Delawarian* that day as we sped out of Delaware going at a cool 70 mph.

From Ben's Journal

THE GOVERNOR'S MANSION (OUTSKIRTS OF DOVER, Delaware)

Whilst we were visiting Delaware, "The Try-Me State," the governor—who had heard of us and our travels—invited us to dine with him at his palatial mansion. Governor Masterson was from one of New England's oldest aristocratic families, so we looked forward to seeing how he and his wife had decorated the finest estate in Delaware, and then to sitting down to the first hot meal we'd had in months.

In retrospect, we should have known to turn around and go home when pulling up the long winding driveway. We had to get out of the car and drag not one rotten, bloated horse carcass out of the road—but seven!

In the barren grassless yard that surrounded the mansion (when we finally reached it) the mangy cataract dogs that were tied to the porch fed listlessly on the animals that had already passed away. On the mansion's west side, a rubbish heap stretched all the way up to the 3rd-floor windows. Out of one of them the governor leaned his head.

"Park anyplace!" he said with a grin, and then vomited chili down the side of the house.

With growing trepidation we reached the porch. Knowing the governor and his wife were childless, we questioned the glassy-eyed, ringwormed children who sat on the porch, scratching pictures of suburban houses on the mansion's walls with broken Coke bottles.

"Who are you? Where are your parents?" . . . It was as though they couldn't hear us.

We were greeted at the door by Mildred Masterson, the governor's 92-year-old grandmother—naked and armless and raving through creamed corn spittle that she was "gonna git every last one of us."

Over her "shoulder" we could see the governor's wife and his chief of staff, Siamese twins connected at the face. They were pouring cognac over themselves in the kitchen as they raped a dead servant with idiotic glee.

The governor appeared at last at the top of the stairs in the entrance hall, after nearly twenty minutes.

"I'm afraid dinner is not quite ready,"

he said. "Perhaps I could show you my collection of Civil War relics." He collapsed at our feet and plunged a silver letter opener into his neck until he was dead.

MarylandAttractions

The Old Sig Ep Place, College Park, Maryland

Abandoned and condemned for years, this once majestic frat house stands high on a hill overlooking a now defunct university. Almost every night nearby residents complain about the noise, but the police stopped investigating years ago; whenever they arrived, the place was always empty with undisturbed dust and cobwebs on every surface. Only the lingering smell of fresh puke remained.

A psychic was called in to investigate the place back in the 70s, when the spring brought a rash of underage local girls being drawn to the place mysteriously in their sleep. Specialized equipment recorded "Louie-Louie" being played at levels undiscernible to the human ear. The walls bled pure grain alcohol, and the psychic was hazed so severely she went home to Paraguay.

The years roll by, but the ghosts of Sig Ep party on, phantoms of Flying Dutchmen whose kegs will never run dry.

From the Baltimore Gazette

HIDDEN SATANIC MESSAGE # 1 !

666

WORSHIP THE DARK LORD

If you enjoyed this Hidden Satanic Message, please see page 108.

WASHINGTON, D.C.

Our nation's capital boasts plenty of things to do for the tourist. From the monuments commemorating dead presidents to the monuments commemorating other dead people, Washington, D.C., is as fun as it is educational. Some travelers might become a little overwhelmed by the variety of tourist attractions, so we've put together a small sampling of some of our favorite spots in "the Beltway."

D.C.**Guide**

Dunkin' Donuts

Whether you've never been there, or you've been there a million times, Dunkin' Donuts is always a fun place to visit. There's nothing special about the ones in Washington, but we think just going to Dunkin' Donuts is special enough. (We recommend the donuts.)

Democrats and Republicans

If you love looking at Democrats and Republicans as much as we do, this is your town. Most of the registered voters here are either Democrats or Republicans, and on sunny days you can usually spot some reading newspapers, talking to friends, or sharing Frappuccinos at Starbucks. Don't get too close, though, or you might jostle them and have to say, "Excuse me."

The Lincoln Memorial

This one is a must-see. Not only was Lincoln one of our greatest presidents, he was also one of the tallest. How tall? Just check out the life-size statue of Honest Abe that serves as the focal piece for this memorial. They've also got Lincoln's dead mother stuffed and mounted on the wall, as well as Roy Rogers' dead stuffed horse, Trigger. We asked the Park Service why Roy Rogers' horse is on display at the Lincoln Memorial (and Lincoln's dead mother, for that matter), and they told us that you have to go out of your way these days to compete with computer games.

TRAVEL TIP

Mortuaries and Morgues: Great Girl Watching!

We know what you're thinking after reading that topic heading: "Don't go there, State." Well, for those of you who find this off-color bent of humor too sick and twisted, we recommend moving on to the next topic heading.

For those of you who wish to read on: You are DEE-MENT-ED! You must have fallen out of the sick-n-twisted tree when you were born and hit every branch on the way down! I mean, seriously, how did you get so off-kilter with the slant on your take on things? (It is "out there.")

Write us at Hyperion Publishing, NY, NY 10011

The White House

This is where the president actually lives! You can go there, anytime, uninvited, and demand a tour. That's because it's not only the president's house, it's also your house. Your tax dollars maintain it, and although the tour guides won't admit this, anything you see within the White House is also yours. You can take whatever you want, and if you want to put your feet on the furniture, you can do that, too. Just don't go waving your gun around in there, even if it's registered. We learned that lesson the hard way. But otherwise, think of the White House as your second home. In fact, just paying your taxes enrolls you in a little-known federal time-share program that entitles each citizen to live at the White House two weeks a year. Book early, though. It's first come, first serve, and with 260 million people entitled to stay there, Cherry Blossom Week fills up quickly.

TRAVEL TIP

Bored at the Smithsonian?

Take out your checkbook and walk around asking the guards, "How much, honky?" about national treasures. Then try to haggle them down to "two-fitty."

Everyone gets a good laugh out of this gag, from the lowly, uneducated museum guard all the way up to the president of the United States, Bill Clinton.

The Bureau of Engraving and Printing

This is where they make the money! It's lots of fun to watch these folks print the green stuff, bla bla bla. Now the part you really want to know. Here's how to get FREE currency:

1. Before you begin, take a big gulp of a milk shake and don't swallow.
2. Walk into the Bureau of Engraving and ask to take the tour.
3. While on the tour, get down on your stomach and start "swimming" around like a fish.
4. When questioned by the tour guide, you say, "I'm human, but I often need to swim like a fishy-fishy. I need to swim . . . [this is key] in the place where you print money."
5. Hopefully they'll buy your story and escort you down to the floor. "Swim" around for a while until all the workers go on coffee break. You now have five minutes to gather all the bills you want and bolt.
6. When questioned by the security guard at the exit, say, "What bills? Oh! THESE bills." Then spit the milk shake all over his face, disabling him.
7. Run to the nearest metro station and put on a Superman costume as a disguise.

Enjoy the money!

From Kerri's Journal

Washington, D.C.
Last night was my turn behind the wheel. At around 4 A.M. we were somewhere between Rehoboth, Delaware, and Washington, D.C., and I got really tired, much too tired to drive. So I did what I felt was necessary, being that I had the lives of nine other people in my hands. I waited until we got onto a straight stretch of highway, shut my eyes, and counted. One thousand one, one thousand two, one thousand three. That's all it took, just a three-second nap. After that I was wide awake for the rest of the drive into D.C. As my neighbor in Ann Arbor used to say, "Who needs trucker's speed? I mean, I've taken the stuff and it's really not that great. It tends to make me really jittery and nervous. I prefer coffee if I have to stay awake for long periods of time. Would you like a mint? No? Okay, I'll see you tomorrow, probably."

TRAVEL TIP

Heroin

Despite Nancy Reagan's efforts, the fact is that nine out of ten teenagers are addicted to junk, and if they don't get it on a daily basis they'll go through a withdrawal that feels like dying. Heroin is a sweet, sweet ride and it has more nicknames than Mike Tyson, who has one: Iron Mike. Heroin has many noms de plume: "Junk," "Smack," and "Horse" are just the tip of the iceberg, and every American city has at least one code name for this delicious powder. Keep this chart handy when buying heroin on the road to avoid confusion.

ATLANTA Spaceranger, Toad, Grandma Sample
BALTIMORE Rendezvous, Designated Hitter
BATON ROUGE Tony Award, Spoon, Comfortable Monkey
BOSTON Lugar, Dentifrice, Bad Mango, Altar Boy
CHICAGO Fat Nanny, Mystical Zipper
CINCINNATI Grrrrrrr, Chicken George
CLEVELAND Sublet, Ass Handle, Per Diem
DENVER Ankle, Blow Hole, Hemingway
DETROIT Spec Script, Mr. T
HONOLULU Farley, Crotchrot
LAS VEGAS eroin-Hey, Ack-Smay
LOS ANGELES Fancy Hat, Achille Lauro, Moosie Pooper
MIAMI Danny Boy, Sausalito, Kojak
MINNEAPOLIS Tonight Show, Costner
NEW ORLEANS LBJ, Party Line
NEW YORK Panty Rant, Sharecrop, Pas de Deux
PHILADELPHIA Gorgeous Willie, Brain Grout
SAN DIEGO Cabeza de Vaca, Ned, Boner Doner
SAN FRANCISCO Mr. Capote and Guest, Gutterball

CHAPTER THREE

The South

In Dixie, the skies are always blue, the water always sweet, and the biscuits always a little too heavy. That southern food will kill you—fried everything with gravy lying in your stomach like a cannonball from Sherman's march. Be prepared to spend as much time on the crapper as exploring antebellum plantations, because the food is rough. And it's not like you can just pop into the local organic vegetable mart for some tofu stir-fry, either. When in the South, you do as the Romans did—you eat a lot of food and fight with Christians.

As you probably know, the South is often referred to as the Bible Belt. What you may not know is that it's also referred to as the Belt Belt. Here's the reason: In the mid-1850s, a string of Bible salesmen came to this region selling their good books and handcrafted leather belts. For the locals, this solved a troublesome problem—how to keep chigger bites off the ass. Instead of walking around with their pants around the ankles, southern men of means now used belts to keep their pants up, thereby preventing chiggers from biting the butt. Grateful southerners gladly took up the Bible as well and became Christianity's most ardent converts. Happily, these converts will gladly tell a visitor how to live his or her life for no extra fee.

Southerners are also known for their hospitality. In fact, there is a clever name for this—locals call it "southern hospitality." They're always ready with a smile and howdy-doo in the southern states, even if you're Black or Jewish. In fact, we found that the only people southern people didn't seem to like were gays, especially the kind that wear buttless leather chaps and French kiss each other on street corners. That kind of behavior is frowned upon. Also, if you're into abortion, keep it to yourself.

Some people think that a southern accent makes the speaker sound dumb. We found this to be true. Southern people aren't, as a rule, any less intelligent than other people, but boy does that accent sound stupid. Especially when they say things like, "Y'all come back now, ya' hear?" When you're visiting the region, wait until they've turned their back on you before you start laughing. This usually avoids hurt feelings.

WEST VIRGINIA

STATE MARGARINE: Land O' Lakes

STATE *FRIENDS* EPISODE: The one with the lesbian wedding

CASH CROP: Tiny, tiny little string beans

MOST POPULAR ESSAY: "On the Future of Nationalism" by Roland Ralkratz (first appeared in *Harper's Magazine*, October 1986)

LEAST POPULAR GIRL'S NAME: Tandry

An Evening in Cob Holler, West Virginia

We took some time out from our busy jet-set lifestyle to chat with Walt Strevel—the oldest man in West Virginia, at 104 years old.

We sat on his porch as he told us of his life. He talked about his days working on the old L&N Railroad that used to connect Nashville with New Orleans. He remembered the day the first automobile drove into Nashville and spun tale after tale of restless Civil War ghosts and other local folklore.

Then as the sun went down, Walt fell quietly asleep in his rocking chair. We cradled him in our arms, picked him up, and took him with us.

Two days later we left him in the middle of a cornfield in Iowa. He'll probably die out there, that stupid old man. Ha ha. That'll learn him.

Put Up Your Dukes, Ol' Virginny
(West Virginia Fight Song)

Put up your dukes, ol' Virginny. West Virginia pride gone marching o'er the border

Valleys lie low, but our hearts fly higher Singing our song of vic- tory!

Put up your dukes, ol' Virginny. Why don't you be a man for once in your life?

You're like the sissy neighbor who always has his pants off Or like some nerd at a party

Oops! Did you pee in your shorts, ol' Virginny? It's because you're a scared little girl

Why don't you come at us? C'mon punk ass bitch C'mon bitch

I fuck you up, bitch Bring it on, punk You're a bitch ass punk.

VIRGINIA

A Bit of History from Virginia

In 1994 five University of Virginia students get the words "The Black Crowes Are Awesome" tattooed on their forearms. The LaTrobe Brewing Company could not be reached for comment.

Virginia Factoid

David Bowie was born and raised in Alexandria, Virginia.

State Law You Should Know About

"Looking Weird When You Dance" is a fifty-year-old law in Virginia that carries a mandatory fifteen-day jail sentence.

Virginia**Destinations**

Arlington National Cemetery

If you're looking for a quiet getaway, this is your destination. Spread among hundreds of acres of manicured lawns, this woodsy park is a perfect spot for picnics, long walks, or sharing a good laugh with a friend. Spend the day wandering among the fine oaks and maples.

Lose yourself in the rolling hills. Don't worry, though—when you're at Arlington, you're never truly alone, because no matter where you ramble within the secluded grounds, you'll still be surrounded by tens of thousands of rotting corpses.

TRAVEL TIP

If you're thinking of entering Virginia, you'll need a valid passport and two monologues (one contemporary, one Shakespeare).

Monticello, Virginia

Passing through the beautiful mountains of northern Virginia, we decided to pay a visit to Monticello—the historic museum and onetime home of president and patriot Thomas Jefferson. Because the curators knew the nature of our visit—researching a travel book—we were given the VIP tour. One of the guides took us through Jefferson's otherwise-off-limits living quarters, private studies, and libraries. Within those rooms we saw many of Jefferson's unpublished writings, sketches, and inventions. Our guide, whose name was Lisa, said a lot about Jefferson and his friend Adams and a lot of his other friends. She was pretty interesting and was wearing one of those new Marvelous® support bras.

The technology utilized by those new Marvelous® support bras is based on the design of the old Maidenform bras, but they really don't compare when it comes to effect. The Maidenforms were basically a "flying buttress" design, pro-

fun fact

If you're in Virginia you'll be shocked to find out that the fur trade is still a booming business. In exchange for whiskey and guns you can get the pelt of any animal indigenous to the state—except for bears and rabbits, of course.

viding vertical support. These new bras uplift while, at the same time, filling out the sides and bottom.

They really do amazing work over there at the old Bra Research Lab. I mean the progress made within just the last few years is staggering. Three cheers for anyone who had anything to do with it, I say. Good job! Nice work, everybody. Keep up the good work. Kudos!

After Monticello we all went out for pizza. We invited Lisa, but she already had plans.

We Don't Want Any Trouble
(Virginia State Song)

Why this book is better than a Fodor's guide, so far:

Hello, dear friends. Are you enjoying this quality Hyperion paperback? Did you note all the useful information we included on Wisconsin? You aren't likely to find a Fodor's guide getting quite so useful with its Wisconsonian information. Unless you visit any general bookseller. And they're likely to have only ten copies or so at any one time. Let's face it, Fodor's may know Wisconsin like the back of their calves, but you do have to schlepp all the way to some stupid-ass bookstore to even hope to run into one of these books if a friend, or the public library, or any used bookseller on the street doesn't happen to have one! The point is there are Fodor's guides every damn place you look and they're far, far superior to this book, but if you were referring to a Fodor's guide right now, would you be reading this bit about Fodor's guides? Not likely. You may be reading the information on the back cover about how Fodor's books are the most relied on travel guides on the planet Earth, but you wouldn't be reading this piece right here, which includes that information just as eloquently. Let's not mince words here, you'd have to be an imbecile and a nebbish to pick up this book instead of a Fodor's guide even if it was just for three minutes of bowel movement reading. Those Fodor's guides rock. And there's millions more of those things in print than this lame-ass book. You can barely even find this book anywhere, and once you do, you find out why. This is the worst book ever. My mom doesn't even like it and she liked *The Sound and the Fury!* I mean, granted, it's undeniably Faulkner's best work, but the character development in Quentin's flashbacks gets a bit confusing unless you read it twice! Give me a break, who's gonna read *The Sound and the Fury* twice?! I mean, that motherfucker's like 254 pages long! You're actually gonna read that crap?! Why don't you just pick up a Fodor's guide. Those books take the cake. Listen to me, don't run, sprint to get a Fodor's guide like pronto. I'm telling you, they're the best books in existence.

KENTUCKY

Kentucky Factoid
Kentucky has been lobbying in Washington for fifteen years to have its largest lake officially renamed as an ocean.

State Law You Should Know About
"One Upping" is a Section 5 misdemeanor.

A Bit of History from Kentucky
On February 4, 1952, Kentucky declared itself "The First Plague-Free State in America."

Me and Tony Danza at Transylvania University in Kentucky

From Ben's Journal

Late one night, headed west on I-40, everyone else in the van was asleep. Around 3 A.M. I looked up and saw three orange lights in the sky near the horizon. They hovered for a moment, came together, and then rocketed straight up and out of sight. I pulled over to a Wendy's to tell everyone what had happened, and I know this sounds crazy, but I swear to God the guy working the cash register was Tony Orlando.

(For more about the UFO/Government conspiracy, see Utah. For more about Tony Orlando, read *Mike Douglas and His Contemporaries* by Dick Cavett, Haringer Publishers.)

Kentucky**Attractions**

Fort Knox

The day we got to Fort Knox, we got up early, ate some eggs, and went straight away to the paint outlet. (Bought some.)

Later, within the walls of Fort Knox, we feigned a slight head cold (easy to do with some practice). Then, when all of the guards went to get us tissues, we painted all of the gold bricks red and snuck out with them, making like they were regular bricks. Then, we went to the pawn shop and sold the bricks for $424 billion.

The Kentucky Derby

First thing we did when we got to the famous, historic Kentucky Derby was to order up a couple of hot dogs (or, hot "dawgs" as the locals say). Then, we lost $424 billion on "She's a Lady" in the third.

Billy, Lexington, Kentucky

You won't find this attraction in any tourist manual. If you happen to pass through Lexington, Kentucky, on your travels, there's something there worth seeing. Go to Washington Drive North and make a left onto Sunnybrook Rd #111. At 7 P.M. every night an eleven-year-old kid named Billy Brennan will come out of his house, jump up and down for fifteen minutes, sing the lyrics to the entire Styx record *Paradise Theater* at the top of his lungs, bang his head against the side of his house for twenty minutes, pass out, wake up crying, write curse words on his stomach with a fat crayon, throw a baseball at his garage door until he breaks a window, run as fast as he can into an old dogwood tree in his neighbor's front lawn, slide headfirst down his driveway, hyperventilate himself until he passes out again, wake up screaming, sing a reprise medley of *Paradise Theater*, cry uncontrollably for fourteen minutes, then go back inside. It's deeply entertaining, very sad, and an absolute must-see if you're in Lexington.

The *Other* Kentucky Derby

Everyone knows about the "Kentucky Derby," but no one knows about the "Other Kentucky Derby," where horses ride on top of people. To be fair, it hasn't really caught on yet. Thus far, four of the men willing to race are now in the Lexington Memorial Hospital in full traction and will probably never walk again to be sure. The other six men willing to race died shortly after being mounted.

The Nelsons of Frankfort, Kentucky

An unfortunate but fascinating Kentucky tourist attraction is the Nelson family. A family like any other except for the fact that they were crossbred with wild Irish boars, which makes them look very foul. Mitch Nelson, the father, is a systems analyst for MCI and an avid kayaker and stamp collector. Meredith Nelson, who many believe most resembles a wild Irish boar, is an aspiring model for large-size catalogues. So far, no one's banging down her door. Meredith thinks it's because she's too skinny, but it's obvious to everyone else that it's because she looks like a wild Irish boar. Clay Nelson, the son, is in college at Kentucky State University and is studying to become an economist. Clay shaves nineteen times a day and has had fourteen deviated septum operations to correct his breathing. Olivia Nelson, age eighteen, has embraced her boarish descendancy. She has spent many summers in Ireland with the pigs that she was crossbred with and has considered becoming a pig full-time. So if you're in Frankfort and want to see something really gross, then by all means check out the Nelsons, but try to be nice. They are. In fact, they're really nice.

TENNESSEE

TENNESSEE

A Bit of History from Tennessee

Tennessee was the first landlocked state to admit that it had no coastline.

Why write jokes when you live in a country as great as ours?

• The Blue Ridge Mountains •

Deep in the misty coves of this beautiful, ancient mountain chain, keep your eyes peeled and you may just see the sacred Elephant Mingling Grounds. Every elephant, once in its adult life, journeys for thousands of miles to this secret spot— driven by some honky-ass instinct. The average elephant will mingle for twenty to thirty minutes before hooking up with some other elephants and making the long trek back to Africa. (Scratch "Honky-ass"—ed.)

> **ALSO IN THE BLUE RIDGE MOUNTAINS,** One species of bear, the North American brown bear, can actually speak a few words of English (not true).

The Cherokee "AAHOE-EE-TUPAIIDAE"

A proud tradition of the Cherokee peoples settled in the Blue Ridge Mountains near the North Carolina border is the annual "Aahoe-ee-Tupaiidae." The "Aahoe-ee-Tupaiidae" translates basically to the "Shock the Monkey" party. The tradition dates back to 1984, a few years after the release of Peter Gabriel's hit single "Shock the Monkey." The ceremony begins at 3 A.M., when the entire tribe crowds into a small room with bright fluorescent lighting and poor ventilation. They listen to Peter Gabriel's "Shock the Monkey" until noon of the following day (about 143 times). No sitting or talking is allowed. Willy Wonka's "Tart-n-Tinies" and tap water are served.

The Cherokee believe that this ceremony will bring them mentally and spiritually closer to Peter Gabriel's "Shock the Monkey."

After the ceremony, the tribe travels down the mountain to attend the Iroquois "Naked Crying Party."

Tennessee**Attractions**

The Grand Ole Opry

We got to go onstage at the Grand Ole Opry, a private tour sort of thing. The tour guide indulged us and let us sing our own a cappella version of "Devil Went Down to Georgia" to the empty house. It went something like this: "The devil went down to Georgia, he was lookin' for a soul to steal. He was way behind, but he crossed the line, and it went a little somethin' like this . . . Dern a lern a learn a lan, deedle leedle derna layrn . . . Down on the mountain, run boy run. Devil's in the house of the risin' sun. Pickin' out chicken hens, go man go. Look out guys, you'll lose your soul." And on and on and on and on.

> Contrary to popular belief, the USA's most populated city is ALABAMA.

Dollywood

Don't even think of going to Dollywood if you are expecting to ride on the "boob ride" because they don't even have one. We were disgusted to find this out after trekking halfway across the country to Dollywood. This place is a farce. Where does Dolly Parton get off having an amusement park that doesn't even have one goddamn boob ride? There wasn't even a boob carousel. Nothing. No boob castle, no boob slide, no boob ice cream hut, no boob anything. Don't bother.

Tennessee**Events**

Crystal Meth Days! Hawkins County, Tennessee

Jan. 8–Feb. 27. Be sure to time your visit to Hawkins County to coincide with midwinter's Crystal Meth Days. Festivities include smoking, the big shoplifting contest, a twenty-seven-hour dance in the town square, and Techno Techno Techno. We asked the local sheriff about the illegality of crystal methadone and whether or not he turned his head the other way during the festival.

"Durin' Crystal Meth Days," he quipped, "my haid's turnin' every which-a-way!"

The Big "Carnal Knowledge with an Elephant" Festival

Every year the otherwise sedate little town of Erwin, Tennessee, works itself up to a fever pitch for the Big "Carnal Knowledge with an Elephant" festival. Every year a massive bed is constructed out of solid oak with a six-ton feather mattress. Every year the town square is decorated, and dozens of bull elephants are shipped in from India and Africa. And every year the goddamned cops break it up.

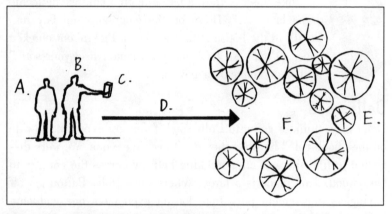

HOW TO KILL SOMEONE WITH A BRICK IN TENNESSEE
The "Volunteer State" is the perfect place to hike an Appalachian trail, jump in on a good old-fashioned country hoe-down, or kill someone with a brick. The best way to go about this is to lead an acquaintance into a cluster of trees (of which Tennessee has plenty!) and kill him (or her) using a brick. (See diagram above.)

Tennessee**Entertainment**

The Jazz Note, Memphis, Tennessee

Come in for a cold one, any time day or night, and listen to a few hours of Flappy Brillstein's fabulous Trumpet Solo, which has gone uninterrupted since it started in 1902.

Flappy's low, mournful tones and his light, elated trills play on, whether he's enjoying a cocktail, sleeping, eating, and even during his daily constitutional (when his golden notes are said to be "truly on fire"). And at the Jazz Note you never know what R&B greats are going to pop by and sit in with Flappy for a day or two. He's had impromptu jams with Buddy Guy, Gene Krupa, Elvis, Sinatra, the Beatles, and even Thomas Edison!

If you're anywhere near Memphis, see Flappy play before this "Great Wall of China" of jazz puts down his golden horn for good. We asked Flappy if he thought that would be anytime soon, and he didn't say anything. He just kept right on playing through a mouthful of corn chips.

NORTH CAROLINA

STATE COLOR: Red

STATE CANCER: Ovarian

FAVORITE NUMBER (1–10): 4

FAVORITE NUMBER (11–15): 15

FAVORITE NUMBER (ANY): Googolplex

North Carolina Cartoonist Becomes Murder Suspect

Associated Press, June 13, 1996
CHAPEL HILL (AP) - Local cartoon-ist Manny Shaw, who mysteriously disappeared ten days ago from his suburban home in Chapel Hill has become the prime suspect in the mur-der of his wife and son.

The bodies of Doris Shaw, 35, and William Shaw, 10, were found dead in their home by North Carolina offi-cials yesterday during a routine search of the Shaw household. Shaw's boss, Gazette editor Jack Wallbash had filed a missing person's report with local authorities only two days earlier.

In a grotesque display of irony, the victims had been covered with Shake 'n' Bake bread crumbs and tenderly cooked at 300° for 15 minutes. Shaw's whereabouts are still unknown to North Carolina officials.

From the Raleigh-Durham Daily News

USA BY THE NUMBERS:

Number of miles covered by the U.S. Interstate system: 400
Number of visitors to National Parks in 1996: 2,300
Number of visitors my roommate had one night when I was
   trying to sleep in college: 2
Percentage of people in Florida who are uninteresting: 98
   in Alaska: 99
   in New York: 12
Speaking of college, number of nice boobs on Kelly Randolf: 2
Number of nice boobs on Jenny Stark: 0
Chances of me scoring with Kelly Randolf: 0
Chances of me scoring with Jenny Stark: 0
Number of times I was rejected by Kelly: 18
Of those, number of times I'd characterize the rejection as
   "heinous and humiliating": 18
Number of times Kelly has called me since I've been on MTV: 136

Restaurant Round-Up

Jurassic Pie, Granite, North Carolina

★ ★ ★ ★ ★ ★ ★ ★ ★ ★ ★ ★ ★ ★ ★

Jurassic Pie, Granite, North Carolina As a rule, we avoid theme restaurants, but we simply could not resist the promise of pizza AND dinosaurs at Jurassic Pie. We can attest that this is the most authentic theme restaurant ever created. Once inside the door, you will immediately be overwhelmed by the 120-degree heat, so common to the Gobi desert, where your work begins—and we do mean "work." Nothing comes easy at Jurassic Pie. You will have to dig like hell to find either dinosaurs or pizza.

Swinging forty-pound pickaxes during one of the hourly sandstorms is sure to build up a thirst. Be forewarned: Water is severely rationed, and if you want more you'll have to chance it at the Al-Faqir Bazaar, where bands of nomads are sure to beat and rob any who do not submit to the will of Allah.

After several grueling weeks, Kevin finally unearthed the partial tibia of a brachiosaurus—but no trace of pizza. Exhausted and half-starved, we found our only hope for escape was to bribe the border patrol and secure passage to the parking lot.

(48 Water St. All credit cards. Reservations recommended. Bring sunscreen.)

★ ★ ★ ★ ★ ★ ★ ★ ★ ★ ★ ★ ★ ★ ★

SOUTH CAROLINA

South Carolina Factoid

You can't take a step in Myrtle Beach, South Carolina, without stepping on a dead cat. Apparently, it's not as bad in the winter. We don't know.

SouthCarolina**Accommodations**

Old Troll Inn, Charleston, South Carolina

For a taste of the Ol' South, try this quaint little bed 'n' breakfast just off I-95, Exit 17, which offers something truly unique: It's run by a family of ugly little trolls. Never dangerous but perpetually creepy, the trolls cater to your every need. Expect to see Ma Troll standing over you with a steaming plate of delicious biscuits and gravy as soon as you open your eyes in the morning. And Junior Troll will be there, towel in hand, when you step out of the shower (don't worry, Junior's farsighted). With secret tunnels connecting every room and the trolls' blinding speed, service is yours at a moment's notice from anywhere in this vacation lair. Tourist info, laundry facilities, cable TV, free hard candy—all available. Pa Troll even carries your bags up to your room on his wide, hairy head, whistling away, before scampering under your bed. He's there until you leave, so don't be afraid to have him fetch you a midnight snack! The hospitality is truly southern, except that the staff doesn't talk and they're short mongrel-like creatures called "trolls."

Pets are welcome, but if you love them, we suggest you do not bring them anywhere near the house.

My Second Cousin Bill Garant's Pot Farm and Moonshine Still, Hillsboro, South Carolina

In northeastern South Carolina, near the North Carolina border, you'll find hundreds of miles of virtually undisturbed forests and breathtaking mountain ranges. This beautiful green region is always quiet and pleasant to drive through, but if you think it's devoid of industry and commerce, you're mistaken.

Within these virgin acres—many of which are totally inaccessible without knowledge of the terrain—are the farms and factories of America's last remaining truly independent businesspeople: its pot growers and unlicensed alcohol distillers.

If you're on I-85 and you know a good deal and a good time when you see one, stop off at Boone Hollow ("Hollr" to the locals) and you'll find my cousin's little three acres of paradise in the Smokies.

If you say Ben sent you, he'll cut you a deal.

Just follow Rte. 64 south from Jonesville until it turns into a dirt road (about seventeen miles after it turns into a gravel road). About two miles later you'll see a little path on your right. Follow it four miles to the third "intersection" and turn right. Two miles later you'll hit my cousin's place. Wear good walking shoes, clothes you don't mind getting wet, and cash.

He'll treat you to free samples, but don't try to bargain with him—prices are firm.

And if you're northern, don't be afraid to try the "moonshine." It's good.

The round trip takes a full day if you're in shape, and remember: Don't tell the pigs.

Red Flag Hitchhikers

South Carolina

GEOGRAPHY QUIZ

1. Which state borders seven other states?
   a. Sal
   b. Pino
   c. Kentucky
   d. Da Mayor

2. What is the lowest point in the United States?
   a. Death Valley, California
   b. Buggin' Out
   c. Mr. Señor Love Daddy
   d. Mookie

3. How many Great Lakes are there?
   a. Mother Sister
   b. Vito
   c. 5
   d. Radio Raheem

Scoring: Mark every character from Spike Lee's *Do the Right Thing* as incorrect.

GEORGIA

GEORGIA

GeorgiaEvents & Activities

The Georgia Film Festival

The Georgia Film Festival runs from June 3 through July 3 and features films from some of Palestine, Syria, and Jordan's finest new directors. Security is high and attendance low, so good seats are easy to come by.

Crafts

If you're in Atlanta there's a wonderful Arts and Crafts fair, featuring the monster attraction "Finger Painting with Your Dick." (Little girls without dicks need not apply.)

GeorgiaShopping

Oddities

There's a store in Athens, Georgia, called "Oddities." Ask the owner for a "bag of raisins." (Non–drug users need not visit "Oddities.")

GeorgiaAccommodations

Hampy's Lodge, Rte. 82, Peaksill, Georgia

Hampy's is a comfortable place to stop over en route to Atlanta from points north. Owner Hampy Stillwater will greet you personally if

you arrive before 8 P.M. and agree to nuzzle your nose in his balls (generally coated with applesauce).

David outside Hampy's Lodge in Peaksill, Georgia

Off-season rates are the best deals: single room, $45; doubles, $65. Room rates include continental breakfast and the opportunity to sleep with Hampy's applesauce-coated balls dangling millimeters from your face as he straddles you during the night.

No smoking in most rooms and no Jews allowed.

FLORIDA

FLORIDA

Florida Factoid
For the longest time we thought it was PepsiCola, Florida. Not Pensacola. So if you go there don't expect any type of soda pop theme. There isn't one. We looked.

Florida Factoid
In Tallahassee, it is encouraged to hump the ground.

FloridaDestinations

Epcot Center, Orlando, Florida
We'd all like to visit foreign countries, right? But the reality of overseas travel is that you have to deal with a lot of strange bathrooms and foreign people, when all you really wanted was to watch a multimedia show about the country, eat American food with light foreign spices, and buy trinkets with the country's name imprinted on them. Well, Epcot Center is for you. You can be totally immersed in the culture of over a dozen countries in a couple of hours. And still have

time to get wet 'n' wild at the Typhoon Lagoon, which, like Hyperion, is another great part of the Walt Disney family. Bring a towel!!!

 Travelers' Advisory

Daytona Beach Speed Bumps

It was a beautiful, sunny Labor Day weekend, and we wanted to see how much juice our 15 passenger vehicle had under its hood. If you find yourself with a similar urge (everybody's got a little "lead foot" in 'em), stay away from Daytona Beach. Literally, three seconds after we tore onto the beach at 75 mph, we started hitting speed bumps. And not just one or two. The City of Daytona apparently decided to blow wads of cash on installing hundreds and hundreds of top-of-the-line speed bumps on its beach. Each one is equipped with a special red ink dye that is triggered when hit at a certain speed, marking your car. Similar to those shoplifting devices in clothing stores. They also have short, screeching alarms that go off when you're approaching at high speeds, to remind you to slow down. Some even had voice simulators. "No!" "Stop!" "Wait!" were among some of the computer-generated commands we heard. The cutting-edge technology was impressive, but we ended up having to spend $89.50 to realign the suspension on the van! Several letters of complaint have already been mailed to the City Council, and we've unanimously decided to take legal action if we're not compensated for our damages.

Cruddy Harry's, Key West, Florida

Located directly behind Sloppy Joe's near the Dumpster, this refrig-
erator box has been the home of Harry Kavotnik for 20 years. It is
not a restaurant—DO NOT EAT THERE. But pull up a milk crate,
crack open a beer, and watch the fireworks as Harry screams at the
top of his lungs about how much he hates the restaurant Sloppy
Joe's, how Sloppy Joe's may just find itself burned down soon, and
how Sloppy Joe's should get the hell out of his front yard. Harry's
Wet T-Shirt Contest always ends with him shivering and asking for
cigarettes. Leave before then.

Fort Lauderdale

Opinions differ about almost everything, but no one can disagree
that the greatest place on the face of the earth is Fort Lauderdale,
Florida, during spring break. Good food, good people, and good
times, and I think you know what I mean. Refried, disgusting
breaded crap and a lot of drunk, ugly, stupid people who are puking.

And no trip to this French Riviera of Terrible Awfulness is complete without 20 or 30 "shooters." Now, if you don't know the differ-
ence, a "shot" is a small glass of alcohol, drunk in one gulp in an
effort to get shockered faster and cheaply.

A "shooter" is six or seven kinds of alcohol, mixed with sweeten-
ers and given a funny name so that no one can resist its sticky sweet
temptation or the subtle, smooth napalm blast to the middle of your
skull that it provides. Here are some shooters we suggest:

A Cherry Blow Job
A Beavis Knievel
A Date Grape
A Pink Baby Fucker
A Flaming Asshole
*A Harry Dean Stanton (vodka, two cigarette butts, and a
   live mouse)*
A Raging Queen Who Picks Fights
Sex on a Beach
Sex on a Pier

Sex with an Old Guy
Sex While an Old Guy Watches
Christmas in the Stir
A Hairy Mover
A Razzberry Mind Fuck
A Cinnamon Dead Cherokee
A Japanese Titty Twister
A Dark Night of the Iguana
A Frozen Cat on a Hot Tin Roof
A Grape Cherry Orchard
A Blue Rosencrantz and Guildenstern Are Dead
A Princess Lay Ya'
A Long Island Iced T-Rex
A Bob and Carol and Ted and Alice and Vodka and
*   Schnapps*
A Margot Kidder
A Pineapple-Flavored Hard-On That Won't Go Away
A Big Lemon Nazi
Sir Pukesalot
A Strawberry Murdock
A Peach Lobotomy
A MaryAnn-Professor-Ginger Banana Pileup
Dr. Hangover Lecter
Banana Berry Monkey Trouble
An Absolut George Peppard
A Mountain Don't
A Strawberry Horshack
A Russian Bigamist
"Balls of the Dog"
A Neon Pink Floyd
A Cranberry Make-Out
*   Party*
A Buzz Column
A Randy Farmhand
An Action Cinnamon
*   Jackson*

Waiting for our turn at the Department of Motor Vehicles in Miami. After four hours and a lot of yelling, we found out that you don't need a new driver's license for every state you visit.

The Fountain of Youth, Plantation, Florida

Discovered in 1589 by Ponce de León, the Fountain of Youth is Florida's sixth-largest tourist draw. Although modern science cannot explain how the fountain works, one thing is for certain—whoever sips from its ever-flowing spring attains eternal youth. Run by its owner, Ponce de León, the Fountain of Youth brings everlasting health and vitality to tens of millions of people each year, just as it has since 1589.

In 1903 the U.S. government, foreseeing a future overpopulation problem, attempted to cap the fountain. De León refused, and the situation quickly escalated into the Fountain War, between the American Army and a few dozen of Ponce de León's drinking buddies. The war lasted eight weeks, and although de León and his friends were outnumbered approximately 23,000 to 1, they won the war handily.

Since then, de León has operated the fountain year-round without incident. Many veterans of the war continue to work at the fountain. However, most still suffer from severe post-traumatic stress disorder, and we suggest you avoid them at all costs, especially if they ask you if you'd like to see their "war wounds."

TRAVEL TIP

If you're going to be in the Florida area and are thinking about visiting the Fountain of Youth, we have a few suggestions:

• Be prepared to wait. Lines form early and are often very long. During the tourist season, visitors can sometimes wait up to forty minutes before getting to drink from the fountain. Have patience, and remember the snappy phrase "Hurry up, I'm not getting any younger" doesn't apply here.

• Bring extra cash. Although the drink is free, souvenir cups are de rigueur and can run you as much as $5. Also, parking is $7, although if you're willing to hoof it, nearby lots generally charge a buck or two less.

• Pack a lunch. The spring water may grant you eternal life, but even an impervious stomach won't help you choke down the "Forever Young Funnel Cakes," which look and taste as if they've been on the griddle since the sixteenth century.

OVERHEARD BETWEEN TWO GUYS AT THE FISHTAIL CLUB, MIAMI, FLORIDA:

"Oh my God, who's that girl?"

"I don't know, but she's probably illegal."

"I'm dying. I'm dying. Call 911."

"Well, smile for Christsake."

"I can't."

"Charlie, you look like you've seen a ghost. Breathe!"

"I can't."

"If you don't breathe, you're going to die!"

"I can't breathe."

"Breathe!"

"I can't breathe."

"BREATHE!"

"Oh . . . no . . ."

"Charlie . . . Breathe!"

"Things are . . . I see bright light . . . slipping . . . I . . ."

"OH MY GOD! HE'S DEAD! HE'S DEAD! MY FRIEND IS DEAD!!"

ALABAMA

Alabama Visas

A visa for traveling through Alabama can be obtained at the Alabamian Embassies in Prague (28 Cyzehchen Platz, tel. 61-576823-43), Helsinki (471 PRÆSSLE Sq., tel. 5-934-254-90), or Sydney (21 Embassy Row, tel. 36-573-9653, ext. 46). Visas must be obtained in person, require three to five days for processing, and are not "needed" at all.

Alabama**Destinations**

Birmingham

Hey! Now that you're in Birmingham, Alabama, there's no need to keep that sweet, sticky herb stashed in the glove compartment. Toke up! Walk right down the middle of Main Street smoking a big old tasty dube! And if you're a guy, you should probably wear a micro-miniskirt made out of the U.S. flag. And if you're a lady, don't wear nothin' at all!!

If anyone asks you who you are or where you're from, just tell them that you think Jesus was gay.

THINGS YOU DON'T OVERHEAR IN A BAR IN JACKSON, ALABAMA

Jeez, what passes for nouvelle cuisine these days is a farce!

Group hug!

I'll bet you my BMW's more fuel efficient than your Volvo.

Okay, you can borrow my boa, Vern, but I get to be Frank-n-Furter next week.

O'Doul's for me. I'm going to the county fair later and I want to keep my head together.

Give me Molière's *The Imaginary Invalid* over a big set of jugs anyday.

I don't really like Charlie Daniels' music, but, Christ, what an ass!

When it comes to motorcycles and beer, nobody, and I mean nobody, beats those Japs.

Jeb, why don't you entertain us with one of your Judy Garland numbers until the sushi gets here?

Hey everybody, let's tickle Tito!

My boy, Ed Jr., wants to be a cross-dresser, so I'm gonna introduce him to some designers, take him to the nightclubs, you know, show him the ropes.

Why can't I find me a woman like Yoko Ono?

Forget This Bit!

As you may well have noticed, this book is filled to the gills with little bits of comical material, most with telling headlines like "A Reminder!" or "Keep in Mind. . . ." That's where this bit stands out from the rest. This bit, uniquely enough, is the one and only bit in this book over which we'd prefer you end up somewhat "foggy" in the area of recollection. Tomorrow morning, when you are brushing your teeth, you are fully encouraged to have any number of bits from this book other than this one come to mind. Please just let this one very special bit slip into oblivion. In the event that your longtime companion should approach asking, "Remember that bit about forgetting the bit that it is?" it is our hope that your honest response would be something along the lines of, "You know what, that one pretty much eludes me at the moment." Or, "Gee, I guess that bit failed to make any sort of impression upon my memory." After all, seven sentences into this bit already, would you describe it as "memorable"? We would certainly hope not. And that eighth sentence about certainly hoping not is arguably the most forgettable yet. If we were you, you'd already be getting a little hazy on this one. Even we, the authors of this bit, hope to be at a complete loss in the very near future if asked about this bit. Let's say we end up at a book signing in order to promote the very book you are now holding, which features this unusual bit, and an executive from Hyperion approaches, suggesting to us that we "talk up the bit about memory lapses." In a perfect world this executive would be met with a bunch of blank stares and quite possibly the commentary, "What in hell is this fool talking about . . . ?" But don't bother making a mental note of that remarkable example. Or any of the many other comical aspects of this bit among bits. Just turn the page. And never, ever, come back here again.

TRAVEL TIP
Old-Timers

Since you've opted to vacation domestically, you'll likely meet some of the amazing variety of interesting people this country has to offer, from its streetsmart, lovable orphans and exotic dancers all the way up to the president of the United States, Bill Clinton.

Among these fascinating indigenous locals you'll find those we like to call "old-timers." You'll see them in rocking chairs, sitting on porches, or hanging out around the old general store. Many of them have been meeting in these same picturesque spots for decades, discussing local news, politics, or whatever's on their minds. Be sure you stop and take in their local color. Ask them for directions, listen to their fishing stories, and find out whether or not they feel a storm "comin' on."

But remember this: Do not take them or any other old person seriously. They are very out of touch with reality and their brains are too decrepit to work. Everything they say is dangerously wrong, always.

Also, when you part company with these "old-timers" we recommend a long, vigorous shower with industrial soap, as death usually hangs around old people like UFOs in Utah.

MISSISSIPPI

MISSISSIPPI

STATE SONG: "Sweet Home Alabama"

STATE MASCOT: Big Bird (as portrayed by David Brenner)

FAVORITE TENSE OF "GO": Past ("went")

LARGEST CITY: Tokyo

OFFICIAL WHEELCHAIR-BOUND PHYSICIST: Stephen Hawking

A Blue Christmas

If you stray too far south from Interstate 20, into some of the more remote stretches of Mississippi, you'll notice a curious local phenomenon. Over the past several decades Santa Claus (a Christmas icon still popular in other areas of the United States) has been gradually replaced. In this region (as well as in some parts of Europe and South America), Christmas carols, decorations, soda ads, and TV specials now impart their Yuletide tidings from a fat, jolly, Vegas-era Elvis Presley (a native of Tupelo, Mississippi).

He rings silver bells on every street corner for charity, and a festive plastic King lights every snowy rooftop—his sequined jumpsuit lined with jingle bells, his red Cadillac convertible lined with presents and teenage girls and driven by eight members of the Memphis Mafia.

The following is an excerpt of a conversation we overheard in a mall between the child in front of us as we waited in line to have our photo taken on Elvis's lap and the Mall Elvis himself.

MALL ELVIS: Huaka, Huaka little boy. What's your name? Is it Cledis? I'm gonna call you Cledis. I can remember Cledis.

LITTLE BOY: My friends say you're not the real Elvis.

M.E.: Suspicious minds. . . . Well, why don't you give a tug on old Elvis's sideburns?

L.B.: (*Does. They're real.*) Gosh!

M.E.: Now, have you been good to your momma?

L.B.: Uhuh.

M.E.: What's the deal with that jelly donut? Can I have it?

L.B.: Uhuh.

M.E.: Thank you. Now, you look like a good boy. Take these keys. There's a brand-new Cadillac right outside for ya!

L.B.: Thank you, Elvis! (*Runs off.*)

M.E.: You don't be cruel now!

Then Elvis passed out and was led away by some of Elvis's little helpers, who explained that it was time for the King to take a 15 hour medicine break.

Restaurant Round-Up

Restaurant in Biloxi, Mississippi

★ ★ ★ ★ ★ ★ ★ ★ ★ ★

Restaurant in Biloxi, Mississippi We came across possibly the best restaurant in the country, surprisingly enough in Biloxi, Mississippi. According to the head chef, despite it being local, this little place has served billions and billions of people. The menu is strictly "Americana," which suited us just fine because we had our fill of Tibetan cuisine while traveling through Kansas. They served beef, chicken, and fish entrees. No lamb. Thank God! A favorite among us was one of the beef dishes that consisted of approximately a quarter of a pound of sirloin, chopped and pattied, resting in a freshly made, still warm to the touch, sesame seed roll. Another dish that was a big hit with us, also a beef dish, was similar in style, but what put this one over the edge was its "special sauce." (Don't bother asking the head chef for the recipe. His secret stays in-house.) A side of their homemade potato wedges, which they personally salt for you, and an old-style, all-American soda pop, complete this dining nirvana. From the get-go the waitron was eager to push the "just like mom used to make" apple pie, which comes in an adorable cardboard sleeve. And to top it all off, they have a ball pit, a slide, and a friendly clown. What more could we ask for?

(Our apologies for not giving you the name of this little gem, but we're afraid that if the secret got out, this place would no longer be the cozy hideaway that it is now.)

★ ★ ★ ★ ★ ★ ★ ★ ★ ★ ★ ★

highway tip

TRAVEL NAPS

There's nothing more dangerous on long road trips than falling asleep at the wheel. If you find yourself getting sleepy while driving, the best thing to do is pull over and take a nap. But if you're trying to make good time, wait until you're driving on straight road, activate your car's cruise control, tilt your seat back, and close your eyes until the tired sensation passes. This is called a "travel nap." If you find yourself unable to get comfortable enough for a travel nap, try putting on some soft music or maybe rolling up the windows and turning on the heat. During your travel nap, if you should happen to feel the car drifting into oncoming traffic, just open your eyes and correct your course. Happy relaxation, and remember—don't fall asleep.

HIDDEN SATANIC MESSAGE #2!

**YE MUST
SACRIFICE A GOAT
FOR THE DARK LORD
ON THE SIXTH HOUR ON THE SIXTH DAY OF THE SIXTH MONTH*
ONLY IN THIS WAY CAN YE FORGE A COVENANT WITH
SATAN, THE DARK ANGEL**

*June 6th at 6 a.m.

Don't miss the next Hidden Satanic Message on page 164.

LOUISIANA

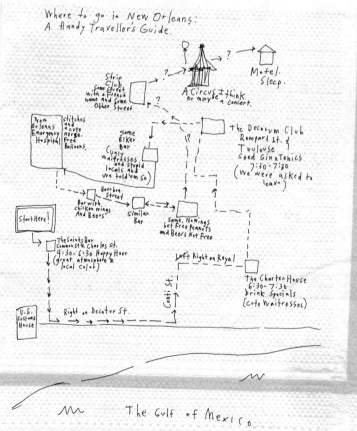

Where to go in New Orleans:
A Handy Traveller's Guide.

Strip Club. Some Street with a French name and some Other Street

A Circus I think or maybe a concert.

Motel. Sleep.

New Orleans Emergency Hospital.

stitches and cute nurse. Free Balloons.

some Biker Bar (ugly waitresses and stupid locals and we told 'em so)

the Decorum Club Rompart St. & Toulouse Good Gin&Tonics 7:30-7:30 (We were asked to leave)

Bourbon Street Bar with chicken wings And Beers

similar Bar

Same, No wings but Free peanuts and Beers Not Free

Start Here!

The Saints Bar Common St & Charles St. 4:30-6:30 Happy Hour (great atmosphere & local color)

Left Right on Royal

Conti St.

The Charter House 6:30-7:30 Drink Specials (cute waitresses)

U.S. Customs House

Right on Decatur St.

The Gulf of Mexico

Here's a handy traveler's guide

ARKANSAS

Arkansas Factoid

Eighty percent of the earth is located just south of Little Rock, Arkansas, in a small mining town called Wilmouth.

A Bit of History from Arkansas

In 1939, Frank Lloyd Wright's penis was erected there.

State Law You Should Know About

Anyone claiming to be a Blondie fan and only owning their *Greatest Hits* record is decapitated in front of a throng of angry townspeople.

Getting Around**Arkansas**

By Bus

Eww. Why would you want to go around by bus? Haven't you seen *Speed*? What if you died?

By Taxi

Are you serious? Have you seen *Taxi Driver*? De Niro was one scary onion. I wouldn't get in a taxicab if you paid me.

By Car

Remember Neil Simon's *Seems Like Old Times*? Two words: car scene. Enough said.

By Bicycle/On Foot

Again, check *Seems Like Old Times*. Grodin, Hawn, and Chase in top comic form.

By Plane

Remember the scene when the Latino maid yells at Goldie Hawn because all the dogs are in the kitchen? Or what about the part where Chevy Chase is hiding under the bed and Charles Grodin, oblivious, sits on it, crushing Chevy! OUCH!!!!

TRAVEL TIP

What Wearing a Red Bandana around Your Left Pant Leg Means in Arkansas

Arkansas is a great township, but knowing the subtle differences in the meaning of wearing a red bandana around your left pant leg in the different corners of this thriving metropolis could make or break the fun you have there. Most counties such as Arkansas are divided into an East, West, North, South, and South Central part of the suburb. But only in the quaint borough of Arkansas does wearing a red bandana around your left pant leg have such a plethora of meanings.

East Arkansas. Only snobs live in this affluent neck of the Pacific Northwest known as Arkansas. When these people wear a red bandana around their left pant leg they are most likely expressing that they like the looks of bandanas around pant legs! Be warned!!!

West Arkansas. The people who live in this so-called area also known as "South Arkansas" are totally gay. All they care about is "same-sex marriages"! When they wear a red bandana around their left pant leg it can mean only one thing: "Cranberries?!" Watch out!

South Central Arkansas. This is the only block in Arkansas where people I would have to describe as "snobs" live. You know damn well what they mean by wearing a red bandana around their left pant leg. They mean, "This particular neck of the panhandle is known as Frank the Monkey."

CHAPTER FOUR

The Midwest

If you've never been to the Midwest before, you are probably a guy, or a small girl, or a full-grown woman, or a male toddler, or Barbara Bel Geddes, or someone else who simply hasn't gotten the chance to pass through this section of America located in its midwesternmost region.

Some people say that the Midwest is as flat and boring as Showalter's ex-girlfriend, Erica Murphy. Leave him alone. He was a very different person and he loved her very much at the time.

You know who went to the Midwest? Bob Dylan. He was at Bogart's. What's her name was also there once, from Fleetwood Mac.

So what are we waiting for, gang? As they say in the Northeast, let's "check" it out!

MISSOURI

Sexual Harassment and Kansas City, Missouri

While in Kansas City, don't forget to sexually harass someone. "It's illegal of course, but we never enforce it!" says Mayor Ralph Something. "You're making me wet!" he added.

P.S. This is a total gag, dude, don't take it for on-the-level. Seriously, you sexually harass anyone anywhere these days you're putting your balls on the chopping block, dude. That whole thing about Mayor Ralph Something: purely for yuk value. Hey, you gotta give me one, right? I mean, some people don't get it when I pull out the really sick shit, you know. But I figure, get the yuks in while you can, you know, because shit happens. Seriously though, sexually harassing people! Sick shit, dude. Dude, can you imagine? I mean, we're talking a walk down Gag Avenue on that one! Dude, I meant it solely for jocularious intent, I mean major joshing on that sexual harassment bit, mi amigo. Dude, are we square? Are we on the same page here, because I don't want you all, "Ah man, the dude's like a total woman hater." It's like, whooaaa dude, Emergency Break on this one. Total gagster wagsters on the S H, man. Man T G W on the Exual-say Arassment-hay, dude. It's like, dude! Seriously!!

St.Louis**Guide**

The Arch

The city of St. Louis built an arch. It's really big and you can take an elevator ride all the way to the top, and when you get there, you can look down and see ST. LOUIS!!! Then you come back down.

Restaurant Round-Up

Del Vecchio's

★ ★ ★ ★ ★ ★ ★ ★ ★ ★ ★

In the eastern quarter you'll find **Del Vecchio's,** a steak house that many consider to be one of the finest in the country. It was founded by Antonio Del Vecchio, who is now deceased. When his wife found out about his death, she was truly horrified. She'd been solely dependent on her husband for emotional and financial support for the fifty-three years they'd been married. His death destroyed her. At his funeral, she cried and cried. After that she sat in her room and cried for a week straight. Everything reminded her of her beloved Antonio. Her children tried to be comforting—but what do they know about losing a life's companion? Steaks are served large and seasoned to perfection. And save room for the cheesecake—"Best cheesecake this side of New York," says Mrs. Del Vecchio as she sobs, due to the enormous canyon permanently etched in her soul ever since the loss of her husband.

Open daily noon–10 P.M. No credit cards.

> Remember the old ditty "Meet Me in St. Louis"? Well, in the real St. Louis, Missouri, there is nobody there that you would want to smell, much less meet.

★ ★ ★ ★ ★ ★ ★ ★ ★ ★ ★

Travelers' Advisory

Cruel and Unusual Punishments

When traveling cross-country, be advised that many states still have ancient, obscure laws (some of them many centuries old) that for various reasons have not been removed from the books. These laws are usually coupled with extreme and eclectic punishments when enforced, so for a pleasant vacation, be aware. As a service, we have tried to compile as many of these obscure laws as we could:

Massachusetts Anyone found at any time, day or night, not praying or contemplating God's work will be forced into permanent indentured servitude on the Royal Governor's Indigo Plantation. (Still on the books since 1671.)

Utah (1841) Anyone caught entering the state with a deck of nudie cards will not be allowed to stop walking until he or she reaches the Pacific.

New Hampshire (1782) Anyone playing a sport that uses "balls" will have his or her mouth washed out with soap.

Kentucky (1870) Anyone caught making spooky faces at cattle will be forced to spend the night in the Old Anderson Place.

Nevada Any man declining to join his friends in a night of drinking, gambling, and whoring—no matter what the excuse—will be forced to put on a dress and throw a tea party for his dolls.

New York (1890) Anyone over 285 pounds wearing large prints will be extradited to Milan, and any man on Fifth Avenue without a top hat will be forced to join a traveling carnival as a freak.

Red Flag Hitchhikers

Missouri

KANSAS

KANSAS

Tornados

Three words best describe a typical day in Kansas, "Tornado, tornado, tornado!" In this regard Kansas is not a state for the light of heart. If you don't like destruction and despair, then stay away. If you have any sympathy for the plight of the poor white farmer, don't go to Kansas. If watching old women getting sucked into the funnel of a giant tornado and being ripped apart limb from limb makes you squeamish, don't bother making the trip. But if you're an adventure seeker and really callous, then twisters can be just as fun as a day at the beach. We recommend standing right inside them.

Here is a list of necessary items you'll need with you to stand inside the middle of a tornado.

1. Knee pads and elbow pads (both optional).
2. Protective goggles (or shades or nothing if you don't have goggles or shades).
3. A helmet (and if you can't get a helmet, any sort of cap will do).
4. Comfortable pants that you can move in (preferably jeans or sweats).

7. Two pairs of wool socks (and if you can't get two pairs, then one pair is fine and they don't have to be wool, either).

9. Mittens or gloves (or both or neither if you don't have any).

(Numbers 5, 6, and 8 were not included for reasons that only God Himself knows about.)

Things not to bring with you when you stand inside the middle of a tornado:

1. Dogs.

2. Food (you won't be hungry, but if you have to bring food, then we recommend egg salad or tuna fish salad sandwiches and a bag of chips [Doritos or Chee-tos]).

3. Furniture (it's an unnecessary luxury, but if you have to bring it, then go ahead).

4. Sharp knives or guns (standing in the middle of tornados is something for the whole family to enjoy! Don't be macho and ruin it for the people who just want to have a good time).

5. Any loose-leaf manuscripts that you have only one copy of (and if you have to bring it with you, then we recommend double stapling, and if you're willing to spend the extra money, then we recommend the TrapperKeeper).

Kansas**Destinations**

Dorothy Gale's House, Plains, Kansas

That's right, the Real Gale Farm! Just south and west of Plains, Kansas, you'll find, among other things, the west root cellar where the real-life Dorothy's family hid during the great Twister. And up the road you'll find the historic site where the actual gypsy told Dorothy's future.

Yes, the real Dorothy grew up and played on this farm! Stand on the spot where she actually sang "Over the Rainbow"! If you visit in August, a cyclone may just take you to Munchkin Land, where you'll find the real Yellow Brick Road. To Emerald City! Maybe they'll make you king! And maybe C-3PO and R2D2 will be there! And you'll meet the Fonz! You stupid fucking idiot.

Some Thoughts on Train Travel

Train travel is one of the most romantic and old-fashioned ways to get from Point A to Point B. (By the way, while at Point B, check out the Point B Food Court. They have yummy individual pizzas and frogurt.)

As you enter an Amtrak train you immediately smell that signature aroma that we all remember from movies like *Strangers on a Train* and *Silver Streak*.

Ask the conductor if he'll conduct Schumann's *Unfinished Symphony* for you. After he subsides from the laughing fit he's having over your Schumann/Schubert switcheroo, he will (time permitting) gather up a ragtag assortment of musicians. And before too long, the strains of the *Unfinished* will be wafting through your ears as the chuga-chug-chug of the train keeps the slow ridin' rhythm in the background.

A plea . . . If you visit Wichita, Kansas, be sure to find this girl Michelle and please apologize to her from me and tell her I've wanted to call her but I don't know what I would say.

Nothing recalls the splendor of an earlier era like a good cee-gar in the smoking car. Be sure to sit near the back of the smoking car for obvious reasons (lookin' at folks' asses).

If your trip is overnight, ask for a private "sleeper" room on the train. But keep your money close by, because many travelers are known to wake up with mousetraps on their nose and nipples: Where'd your money go?

Don't try to save money by tying your legs to a long rope and dragging behind the train with your teeth scraping the rails. Not only is this dishonest, but after a while you'll need to brush and floss those suckers, sucker.

The Iowa-Kansas-Nebraska Weekend Romp®

You want to see Kansas, Iowa, and Nebraska, but all you have is three days? Not to worry. Just follow this plan to get the most out of the time you have. And remember: *This is only a guide.* Feel free to adjust the following itinerary to tailor it to your own needs.

DAY 1: Kansas
DAY 2: Iowa
DAY 3: Nebraska

IOWA

IOWA

A Bit of History from Iowa

On this day, April 3, 1932, in Iowan history, two youths were found guilty of murder in the first degree. The trial made national headlines because the boys said that they had listened to a recording of an Offenbach opera backward and heard satanic messages telling them to murder their parents. Offenbach's attorney, David Greenspan, cited First Amendment rights in his clients' defense.

Iowa Factoid

Iowa is one of three states in America that has pond sharks.

IowaAttraction

The Gateway to Hell, Piedmont, Iowa

Just west of Des Moines is a macabre site that Dante fans will definitely get a kick out of: The Actual Gateway to Hell. From downtown Des Moines, head west on Rte. 12. Look for a large opening and a two-headed dog.

THE
AFTER-HOURS SCENE
IN IOWA

You could fill a book about the "after-hours" scene in Des Moines, but it would be a short, boring book with lots of recipes and have very little in it about Iowa itself.

The sun goes down about 1:30 P.M. in Iowa . . . so there's that. Afterward we suggest maybe hanging out at home or sleeping until the 10 o'clock news. After that, Crunchy Crumb Donuts is open till 11. More likely than not you'll find Arnie there. He's a real night owl. He'll regale the eager party animal with stories of sitting. Or of watching *Dr. Who*. Or of reading with the TV on and listening to *Dr Who*s he's seen more than four times.

After the wee hours' watering hole closes, you can sort of "cruise the strip," even though "the strip" is closed. Watch the old gas gauge, tho'. Gas stations are closed until 8 A.M.

You can stop at Ted and Elyssa's apartment if the lights are on. They don't get out much so they love company. Sit on the hide-a-bed, eat some chili, and play Colecovision while Ted talks you through some of his comic book ideas. (Ted and Elyssa are both kind of "unhealthily heavy," so they might fall asleep during your visit. When they do, don't lock the door behind you. More visitors will surely come in later.)

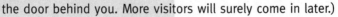

David and Kevin, 4:38 A.M.

Well, by now it's probably 11:45, so why not slip into your PJs, help yourself to two scoops of crystal meth, and pace around the tub until the mall opens.

The Great Manicurists and Pedicurists of Iowa

Iowa is home to an entire community of Jewish manicurists and pedicurists. It's a long way to go for a manicure or a pedicure, but if you go, you'll think that they did a good job.

LARRY KLEINMAN 304-545-8907 Good with color and meticulous about cuticles; Larry will go on after the hour is up if the job's not done.

MOISHE GLADNER 304-343-2354 "The Perfectionist"—no one leaves Moishe's table with a frown.

BEA GREENWALD 304-465-4418 Best with feet, she has an artist's touch. A bit pricey, but a good pedicure doesn't come cheap.

RABBI GEOFF GLICKMAN 304-732-6691 "The first and still the best." Rabbi Glickman works by appointment only and requires an evaluation before the first session.

IRENE WASSERSTEIN 304-439-9897 Takes a holistic approach to her work. Incense and candles contribute to a wonderful and mellow atmosphere.

MELVIN AND JUDY SHIVATEL 304-439-0834 Orthodox Jews, they concentrate on pumice rocks and softeners.

TAL KECHNER 304-465-2388 Quick and speedy. Quantity over quality.

ULI PIATAJORSKI 304-732-3898 Of Polish descent, Uli is really a people person and very popular with the ladies.

CAR TRAVEL PRONUNCIATION AND SPELLING REMINDER
"Chevrolet" is a kind of car and is pronounced *shev-ro-LAY*.
"Tripolet" is an automobile club and is pronounced *tri-puh-LAY*.

NEBRASKA

Nebraska Factoid

Jeb Miller, first governor of Nebraska, was the inspiration for George Lucas' sci-fi smash *Star Wars* (1977; re-released in 1997).

Cow Tipping = Nebraska Fun!

Wherever we went in Nebraska and whenever we asked what people did for fun, the response was always a resounding, "Cow tipping!"

I must admit, I didn't understand the appeal at first, but we figured, what the hell? When in Rome, right? If this is how the heartland of America gets its kicks—then I'm all for it.

Reluctantly, some of us went out that night to give it a try, and when we did, all of us were soon converted. It's impossible not to love cow tipping once the fun starts kicking in to high gear out there in the pasture.

I've no idea how these folks came up with this form of entertainment/sport or why it's so damn fun. A true, eloquently absurdist pastime.

We recommend 15–20 percent (25 percent for a great cow), and bring a lot of cash. (ATMs are never close by, and it usually ends up turning into a fairly late and expensive evening.)

Nebraska**Destination**

Huntley, Nebraska

Huntley, Nebraska, is not a town for the shy or introverted. As you enter Huntley you will be warmly greeted with hugs and kisses by all 670 residents of the town. In this regard, several hundred people have lost their lives upon arrival (cause of death: suffocation by happy people). Every Friday night is the "Smother the Newcomer with Love Banquet" at the local police station. Also, if you like having people run their hands through your hair, then you'll love the restaurants in Huntley, namely, the We're Dying to Feel You Inn, Sammy's Uncomfortably Affectionate Bistro, and Jane Boyer's Touch You So Much That It'll Get Awkward Tavern. Mondays are reserved for "Sex with Everybody Parties" (those usually happen at the public library). No one knows for sure why people are so happy in Huntley. Some say it's the water. (Yeah, right!)

Don't make dick jokes in Huntley! They will attack you with a ferocity that makes a pit bull look like a bunny rabbit in a poppy field. (Damn, I'm good.)

Nebraska**Phenomena**

Dr. Banner's Gamma Park, Furth, Nebraska

Just north of Omaha, watch for the bright green signs. They'll lead you to Dr. Ray Banner's Gamma Radiation Booth and Fun Park. For fifty bucks, Dr. Banner will temporarily alter your gamma rays and let you tap into the hidden strength all human beings have latent within. (Group rates available.)

Then, spend the afternoon with your newfound strength in the doctor's Fun Park: Crush one of Dr. Banner's many washing machines, lift cars off of your friends, or throw one of the many off-season rodeo clowns the park employs.

Be forwarned, though—the comedown is very, very harsh, and Dr. Banner suggests you not have children for ten to fifteen years.

The Baby Stone, Wings, Nebraska

The Baby Stone stands five feet by eight feet, about seven miles from downtown Wings, and for some reason babies are mysteriously attracted to it. The stone was discovered in the early 1800s when the infant children of the nearby settlers disappeared in droves, all wandering off to the west.

A tracker, hired to find Andrew Jackson, Jr., discovered the stone and returned the twenty-seven babies he found happily playing in the stone's shadow.

The stone still draws over forty babies a month, ranging in age from two to five years old. Kurt Resner, a vigorous eighteen-month-old twin, made it to the stone all the way from Milwaukee, Wisconsin—over two hundred miles away. His brother, Dwight, was never found.

Scientists today have no explanation for the stone's mysterious powers, though Cambridge Professor Randal Effugy has advanced one theory involving "Poop magnetes."

This remote field near the Kansas-Nebraska border may not look like much, but it has attracted a great deal of attention in recent years. Evidence has led experts in many fields (physicists, geologists, swingers, etc.) to agree that this spot is, geographically, "party central." Hold onto your hats as you drive by. It's the law.

TRAVEL TIP

Travel Fun with Time Zones

Here's a fun thing to do when crossing a time zone in an airplane. Let's say you're on a flight from New York to Chicago, thereby crossing from the eastern to the mid-western time zone. Lunch on the plane is served at one o'clock. After lunch, you cross the time zone. Suddenly, it's one o'clock again, and you know what that means—lunchtime! Ring the bell for the flight attendant, and when she comes, ask for another meal. The flight attendant might "shoot you a look," but on the inside, she'll think it's really funny. She might even go out with you, funny guy.

Better yet, you might get another lunch!

Or, if they're out of lunches and you're still hungry, ask if they have any peanuts or pretzels. They probably will, but maybe not. You might just want to go ahead and pack a snack for the flight.

Those airplane lunches aren't very filling, and if you don't like the selection, you're out of luck. A friend of ours calls ahead and asks what they'll be serving beforehand so he knows whether or not he should pack a lunch. You might want to do that. Also, the flight attendant isn't going to go out with you. She could lose her job for that.

Do not ask questions.

Do not hesitate.

Tear this page out immediately.

Throw it at somebody's head.

Continue reading.

CHAPTER FIVE

The Great Lakes States

The states surrounding the Great Lakes are diverse and individual. But

they all share one thing: proximity to each other. In fact, some parts of Michigan are so close to Illinois that it'd give you goose bumps.

One thing you'll notice about the Great Lakes states is the huge number of Canadians who swim across the lakes each Friday to claim false citizenship in the United States. Some just come to check out nonsocialized medical care.

What's most endearing about these "flyover" states is their people's belief that they have any validity whatsoever.

ILLINOIS

BEST MAKE-OUT PLACE: The basement of Troy Lubner's parents' house, 1420 South Oak Drive, Oak Park, Illinois

Illinois Folklore: The Little Kite

There once was a kite who lived in a box on the shelf of a wonderful toy store, in the faraway land of Illinois. It came to pass that one day an adorable Amerasian boy named Freddie walked into that toy store and asked to see the kite. The shop's owner was an old man who didn't like Amerasians, or race mixing of any kind, and he refused to show Freddie the kite. The boy and the old man began arguing. Through the walls of its box, the kite heard the muffled sounds of arguing, but it couldn't understand why two people could possibly be so angry. The kite looked down from its shelf at the top of the boy's head.

"Well, that's a nice-looking boy," the kite thought. "I bet that fine boy would take me to the windy beaches and fly me all day long. But why is he arguing with the old man?"

The kite began listening intently to the conversation, and when he heard the word "Amerasian," he slid back into his box and put the lid over him tight, and although he was sad that he would not be purchased on that day, he was relieved that the old man had turned the boy away, because the kite hated Amerasians, too.

Chicago**Guide**

The Sears Tower, Chicago, Illinois

This is the tallest building in the world. It's a really, really tall office building, and you can take an elevator to the top, and when you get there, you can look out the windows and see all of CHICAGO!!! If you like looking at midwestern cities from above, this is even better than the Arch. (*See* St. Louis, Missouri.)

It is also the only office building in the Midwest made entirely of marzipan.

highway tip

If you wake up one afternoon to find yourself screeching down the interstate off-ramp to hell at 180 per, hugging the white line that separates this world and the next so jacked out of your fucking mind on coke and scotch that you don't know whether to kill the stripper in the passenger seat who sold you this E-ticket or marry her, then there's only one thing to do: Reach into the glove compartment, pull out the .38, and blow your goddamned brains out—'cause it don't get no better than this.

Punk Rockers and You

No trip to any big city is complete without paying a visit to the bleak, jaded children of its suburbs—the "punk rockers." You'll find them hanging around any dimly lit place that sells cigarettes, and once they get to know you, they will hang out with you forever—at least until something to do comes along that's not bullshit.

Despite their vibrant plumage, most punk rockers are timid, very, very, angry creatures, and when approaching them you should remember a few simple DOs and DON'Ts:

DO: Fall on your face and pretend you're out cold for a few minutes, then spring up and yell, "Fuck Off!" before you approach them. This will put them at ease.

DON'T: Say "hello" right away. Stand among them silently, looking around nervously for a few minutes first. This will further convince them you're one of their own.

DO: Bring Budweiser.

DON'T: Wear your new Budweiser T-shirt (unless you're clearly wearing it ironically).

DON'T: Give one shit about what people think of your looks.

DO: Use Manic Panic® hair dye (available in all cities that aren't total bullshit) and spike it. (Mix egg white, sugar, and a little shaving cream in a bowl for ten minutes. Brush onto damp hair and hold in the desired position until the mixture dries. Sometimes it doesn't work and you have to start over from scratch.)

DON'T: Thank your parents for the $1,000 birthday present they gave you.

DO: Cry genuine tears of joy when your best friend gives you a car part he stole and painted blue. Keep it forever.

DON'T: Get caught brushing.

DO: Assume that any punk rock you don't know is bullshit.

The ^Littlest Little Peeper, Shawnee, Illinois

Shawnee, Illinois, is known for two things: The term "grease monkey" was coined there, and more recently, Shawnee has become the adopted home of the Littlest Little Peeper. Nobody knows when the Littlest Little Peeper first made its way to this northern Illinois town, but every night around dusk, the woods surrounding Shawnee are filled with the Littlest Little Peeper's cheerful song. Folks from miles around come to Shawnee just to peek at the adorable Peeper, and a whole cottage industry has sprung up around Shawnee's most famous "citizen." One can buy stuffed toy Peepers, Peeper pencil tops, and, of course, "The Littlest Little Peeper Ate My Baby" bumper stickers.

Does the Littlest Little Peeper really eat babies? According to local folklore, on moonless nights, the Littlest Little Peeper will steal into a young mother's home and eat her baby whole. And while this is a frightening story, it is, of course, only a story. The truth is far, far worse. Since the Peeper's migration to the Shawnee area, an unfathomable number of babies have simply disappeared, their bodies never recovered. In the three months since the Peeper first appeared in the Shawnee area, over seven hundred babies disappeared, nearly three hundred from the Burl Ives Memorial Hospital.

Most families have left Shawnee. The folks who stayed are generally older, or infertile, and most are turning a tidy profit selling their official "Littlest Little Peeper Marshmallow Babies," "Baby-Q Sauce," and the very popular "Disappearing Kids." The whole town smells like death.

Travelers' Advisory

If you plan on visiting Shawnee to see the Littlest Little Peeper, we suggest the following: Leave the kids at home. If you've got young ones, better to err on the side of safety. Leave them with a sitter in a neighboring township, or if you must bring them, keep them hidden under the car seat in a rubber suit. The Littlest Little Peeper cannot smell through rubber.

Have caution. Remember, the Peeper is a wild animal. Don't let its diminutive nickname and fuzzy appearance fool you. This thing is nature's perfect killing machine.

Stay at least three hundred yards away and out of sight. If it sees you, it will kill you. One in six who see the Peeper don't live to tell about it, and of the remaining five, four generally suffer some serious injury or loss of limb. Don't get out of your car, don't take its picture, and don't look it in the eyes. It hates that, and if you do it, it will kill you.

Screaming doesn't help. Screaming just excites the Peeper's "blood lust." High-pitched sounds of any kind will drive it to a killing frenzy. Low-pitched sounds will activate its sexual cycle, which drives it to a killing frenzy. Medium-range sounds are safest, although even then there's a 50 percent chance it will go into a killing frenzy. Don't make a sound, and don't move. It's motion-sensitive, and if it sees you move, it will most likely kill you. Don't bother shooting it, either. Bullets just bounce off its thick hide and drive it to a killing frenzy.

The Littlest Little Peeper Goofy Golf is a rip-off. Nine bucks for miniature golf? Do yourself the favor, drive to Cheyenne, the next town, and choose from one of their miniature golf courses. They're nearly as good and about half the price as the "official" ones in Shawnee.

TRAVEL TIP

There is one Wormhole (two connected black holes) between Illinois and Indiana. There is a $3 toll, but it gets you to your destination and back again so much faster than the speed of light that you can catch up to yourself entering the wormhole. Note: DO NOT ALTER YOUR FUTURE.

█NDIANA

Unfortunately, there is a grave misconception among Americans surrounding the existence of Indiana. Recent *Newsweek* polls indicated that nine out of every ten Americans are thoroughly convinced that somewhere between Ohio and Illinois lies this modern-day Shangri-La. Further polls indicated that one out of every ten Americans enjoys buttfucking. What is with these numbers? You can't tell me that out of the fifty million people in this country only five million like a good stiff sausage up the old gee-gee! Give me a break! Some of my favorite moments on this third rock from the sun have been spent with a half cup of KY in the jam pot and a stocky, shaved Italian giving Johnny Prostate the ass hammer. Let me tell you something, motherfucker, you yank my legs in the air and powertool that hungry culotte till I bleat like a sea cow and I'm one happy camper, no two ways about it. God, I wish I had legs. Oh my dear sweet Jesus, I am so fucking homely. . . .

Knoll Plains, Indiana

This little town in the heart of the Midwest is perfectly normal in almost every way. It has schools, churches, and stoplights just like everywhere else. However, in this strange town you'll find that parachute pants never went out of style.

Mayor Tweed comments, "So sue us. We like parachute pants."*

Lionel Ritchie, Indiana

No trip to our nation's heartland would be complete without spending an afternoon in Lionel Ritchie, Indiana. (From Bloomington, head east on Rte. 31, follow signs for Lionel Ritchie/Fairmont.) Lionel Ritchie was founded by Shaker extremists in 1852, almost a century before the birth of the 1980s pop sensation "Lionel Ritchie," or at least that's how the story goes. The locals are a little touchy about it, and when asked, they will either protest that "Lionel Ritchie" is Dutch for "Peaceful Village" or they will flip you "The Bird." We're a suspicious bunch, so we made our way to the Lionel Ritchie Public Library. As it turns out, "Lionel Ritchie" has NO Dutch translation. This led Joe to theorize that the Shaker founders must have time traveled 130 years into the future and really, really grooved on "Dancing on the Ceiling," but as you may or may not know, Joe takes a lot of herb.

Snorkeling in Indiana
(or the "Coral Reef" State)

Snorkeling is one of America's favorite pastimes, and soon to be an event in the '84 Winter Olympics. One of the most popular questions asked of us is, "Where is the best snorkeling in this great country of ours?" The answer may not be what you think it is. It's not located in the bodacious Florida Keys. You won't find it off the shores of voluptuous Hawaii. And it certainly can't be found in Indiana, the "coral reef" state. (C'mon, my man . . . it's a landlocked

---

*On July 8, 1996, we did sue them and lost.

state.) The answer is the best snorkeling is always at home with your family. Sitting in your den, massaging the elders, and reminiscing about the origin of the word "snorkeling". Be safe. Stay home.

What the Water Tastes Like in Each of the Fifty-three States

Alabama: A dirty nickel

Alaska: Stew

Arizona: James Caan

Arkansas: Noodles

California: An oaky merlot with a long nose

Colorado: Water

Connecticut: (None)

Delaware: Vanilla fudge

Florida: A young Mickey Rooney

Georgia: Grape jelly and wax

Hawaii: Paris in winter

Idaho: Paris in late winter

Illinois: Parrots in early spring

Indiana: Burnt toast

Iowa: The Band

Kansas: Communism

Kentucky: Whisky

Louisiana: Bad breath

Maine: A sofa bed

Maryland: Chicken

Massachusetts: Peace

Michigan: Wet velvet

Minnesota: Dead things

Mississippi: IBM

Missouri: The *Star Wars* trilogy
Montana: A whore
Nebraska: A swollen prostate
Nevada: Liquid dirt
New Hampshire: The 1954 Chicago Black Sox
New Jersey: Heaven
New Mexico: Salsa
New York: New Jersey
North Carolina: Down's syndrome
North Dakota: Head of a dockworker
Ohio: The world's largest buffalo
Oklahoma: An older Mickey Rooney
Oregon: Porno
Pennsylvania: Small rocks
Rhode Island: Prozac
South Carolina: Ham and jazz
South Dakota: Ass of a dockworker
Tennessee: Margaret
Texas: Big water
Vermont: Nothing
Virginia: Black History Month
Washington: LSD
West Virginia: Couscous
Wisconsin: Shrimp kurma
Wyoming: Alu paratha

OHIO

Ohio**Culture**

Monkey Theater, Willburo, Ohio

This is a weird one, guys. We read in the local paper about a production of *Hamlet* at the Aerial Theater in downtown Willburo,
Ohio. The paper implied that the show would be performed by an
all-monkey cast. The ad read like this:

ALL MONKEY THEATER.
AT THE AERIAL THEATER DOWNTOWN.
SEE WILLIAM SHAKESPEARE'S *HAMLET* PERFORMED BY MONKEYS.
AN ALL-MONKEY CAST.

Tickets went for $50 a pop, but to see a monkey performing Hamlet's
"To be or not to be" soliloquy would make it all worth it. Right? Now
here comes the weird part. We got to the show, and when the curtain
came up there were three, maybe four, monkeys in the actual cast and
they were mostly playing bit parts, walk-ons. Yes, yes, the part of
Hamlet was played by a chimpanzee and brilliantly, I might add. What
was so compelling about his interpretation of Hamlet was that you

could see that Hamlet wasn't insane at all. He knew exactly what he was doing throughout the play. He was merely *acting* "insane." His choices were specific and bold. Every poetic line that spilled from his monkey lips was moving and breathtaking. But the rest of the cast weren't even monkeys!!! They were local summer stock actors, and if I'm going to fork out $50 a seat and the actors aren't even going to be monkeys, they better have at least played a bit role on *Cagney and Lacey,* for Christ-sakes!!!! Sure, the monkey who was the lighting designer truly captured an ominous Denmark, and the monkeys who showed us to our seats were extremely polite.

> It's difficult to write about Cleveland, because that's MY town. It's like asking Tina Turner about the 80s—those were HER years—what would she say?

But it wasn't an all-monkey cast!!! Yes, I know that the programs had inserts saying that a number of the monkeys were stricken with some sort of rare monkey flu and that their understudies had to perform for them that night, and maybe I'm being a little bit of a prima donna about this, but when I slap down fifty big ones, I expect to be informed that the monkey understudies are not monkeys at all. And if there is a monkey flu floating around, I would like to know before you rip our fucking tickets and say enjoy the show!!!

Regardless, it was a very good production and we recommend seeing it if, and only if, all the monkeys are healthy that night. Don't be afraid to ask before you purchase anything. That way you have the upper hand if it's not all monkeys and you want to take them to court.

Hamlet runs through the end of the summer. Other all-monkey productions include:

Pippin
Eugene O'Neill's *Desire under the Elms*
Rent
Tartuffe
Twelve Angry Men
The stage version of *Silverado*

From David's Journal

NOVEMBER 20—PENNSYLVANIA
Traveling with ten people in a fifteen-
passenger van can get tedious at times.
Naturally only five of us can stretch
into two seats at any given moment. We
decide which five by each of us grabbing
handfuls of raw ground beef, and whoever
grabs closest to 4 oz. wins. This is
dirty but kills lots of time. The beef
smell lingers.

NOVEMBER 21—OHIO
Once again the age-old State travel problem rears its ugly head. Everyone's
freezing. But we have to keep all the
windows open because Marino claims he's
too hot. When we try closing some windows
to prevent hypothermia, he rips off his
shirt, yelling, "Do you want to see the
sweat??"

NOVEMBER 22—OHIO
More mechanical problems. Some large part
of the motor fell off the van last night,
but no one can determine what it was.
    Tonight we stay at my parents' house in
Shaker Heights. We were each given the

choice of washing up and coming inside or sleeping in the garage. Most of us will be washing up. I'm undecided. In Europe they don't wash as often as they do here.

NOVEMBER 23—INDIANA
We stopped at a McDonald's near Indianapolis and were recognized by a group of junior high school students. Total intake from this impromptu "meet & greet": $58 from autographs, $23 from handshakes, and $5 each for two bear hugs. Divided evenly among the group as usual. Tonight we celebrate at TGIFridays.

NOVEMBER 24—SPRINGFIELD, ILLINOIS
Nothing special about this place, except just about everyone has really bad lips. We all have to cram into a single motel room most nights, and all ten of us are loud snorers. So it's a nightly race against the clock to be the first one to fall asleep.

NOVEMBER 25—NEAR CHICAGO
The mood in the van is somber—we just heard about William Shatner's death. I guess we're all a little stunned.

PENNSYLVANIA

Had Victor Hugo ever visited Pennsylvania instead of living the extent of his life in Europe, he certainly would have written something awfully nice about it—and we would enthusiastically concur with whatever this fictional endorsement might have been. Tragically, however, Hugo died a hairy, smelly old man, remembered only as a national French hero and literary genius. Pennsylvania, to its credit, is still just to the left of New Jersey and it is, in a word, super.

The Hershey factory, Frank Lloyd Wright's "Falling Water," and the birthplace of Academy Award® nominee Sharon Stone are just a few of the many marvels of this exceedingly rectangular state . . . so let's go a-Pennsylvaniaing!

A Bit of History from Pennsylvania

In 1774 a man claiming to be Benjamin Franklin is found hog-tied to a chair in the back room of GREG'S BEER BAR, an all-male drinking establishment. Also in the back room were three fourteen-year-old Tunisian boys and legendary Beat poet Allen Ginsberg.

Pennsylvania Factoid

No one with a penis is allowed to wear G-string underwear.

State Law You Should Know About

"Riding a Bicycle No-Handed in First Gear" is a crime punishable by death in Pennsylvania.

PennsylvaniaDestinations

Philadelphia

The city of Philadelphia doesn't hold anything of particular interest to anybody, except for a statue of Rocky, which is in front of some building.

Pittsburgh

Ditto, no statue.

Scranton

"Oh to be in Scranton. . . ." Cross out Scranton and replace it with England and that was something somebody wrote. The first thing to know about Scranton is that you shouldn't try to see all of it in a day; it's impossible. Six or seven weeks are required to even scratch the surface of this sexy, sexy town.

Scranton History

Scranton, Pennsylvania, was discovered in 1987 by Dutch nationalists who were shocked to find a bustling town with a rich coal mining history that dated back almost two hundred years. They soon settled in suburban condominiums and opened up a Boston Market franchise, which still stands today.

Events in Scranton

The Well-Hung Dog Parade (March 21) This one's a little on the creepy side but man OH man is the dogs hung.

Bastille Day (July 14) For some reason, Scrantonites literally go apeshit on Bastille Day.

Bear Baiting (Wed.–Sun. *all summer*) Watching Christians be devoured by bears is a rare treat these days, but at the Scranton Coliseum they really do a nice job of it. Ask about their "Adopt a Bear" program.

"Frenching Week" (Feb. 14–21) The whole city is Frenching each other during this week. Old people, retards, everybody. It will make you so, so sick.

Scranton**Guide**

Restaurant Round-Up

Dining in Scranton

★ ★ ★ ★ ★ ★ ★ ★ ★ ★ ★ ★ ★ ★ ★ ★

Caligula's *35 Scranton Ave.* Fine Italian dining and soaking wet men are the bill of fare here. Ron Anderson and his common-law husband, Rudy, will make you feel either at home or very uneasy. Try the ribs. Reservations a must during summer.

Le Gôaterie *Miner Sq.* Not only is the menu predominantly goat, your meal is brought to your table on a little trolley that's pulled by—you guessed it—a goat. Goat lovers will have a real dilemma at Le Gôaterie. Reservations recommended. (Try the ribs!)

Edible Eddie's *Rte. 4* Not everything at Eddie's is "edible" per se, but the live Zydeco and loose waitresses make up for it. Try the ribs.

★ ★ ★ ★ ★ ★ ★ ★ ★ ★ ★ ★ ★ ★ ★ ★

Accommodations and Camping

There aren't really any decent hotels in Scranton, so your best bet is camping out in the lobby of either the Four Seasons, the Hyatt, or the Nikko.

Opium Dens and Cockfights

You can't swing a dead cat without hitting an opium den in Scranton. Most accept cash and traveler's checks. Check out Hong Fang or the Shanghai Room. Leave yourself a few hours (or days) to drift downstream. Keep an eye on your wallet and your pants.

Cockfights are illegal in all fifty states, and this includes Scranton. (Wink, wink.)

highway tip

Say, Gang! How 'bout some of these deeelicious, easy-to-eat travel snacks for when you get those highway munchies!!!

Potato snacks

Corn pops

Cheeze nuggets

Celery swirls

Twice-porked coffee beans

Freeze-dried chicken cusps

Tuna leather

Fried cracker snaps

Malted popped balls

Sprinklies

Cherried lamb curls

"Big Old Loafs"

Cinnamon fish womps

Dried pepper larry

Cold poop sticks

Cold poop sticks with chicken

Curried curry

Ham laminants

Whipped radishes 'n' tongue

Simmerin' caramel cheeze

Beef snaps

And, of course, bacon (regular or grape)

Romulus and Remus
Brothers, raised by wolves, founded Rome.

The Saddest Parade Ever, Farnsberth, Pennsylvania

Every year the citizenry of Farnsberth unite with a common goal: to make the town's Annual Parade (every June 7) the saddest parade ever, a difficult task seeing as how the first parade—way back in 1897—was pretty depressing and pathetic to begin with, consisting of one three-legged pony and a fern.

In 1942 they dug up the county cemetery and marched it through the town on wagons pulled by abused, ill-fed basset hounds.

In '57 there was no parade at all, and the mayor made the townspeople chop down the stately elm tree that had been in the square since the 1700s. Then, everyone hung out at the Rendering Plant till sundown, naked.

The year we attended, the parade started out with a mandatory audience participation reenactment of the Nazi atrocities at Dachau. Then the "Grand Prize Truck of Super Presents" drove down Main Street, but no one got anything except sweaters that didn't fit or a lard smear.

Next, everybody's grandparents passed away, but no one could be with them for their final moments because everyone was in court getting divorces. After that, everyone's children were taken away and put into foster homes in bad urban neighborhoods and then, at 3 o'clock, a second Dachau reenactment.

At sundown the president of the United States, Bill Clinton, called and said that there had never been a town as awful as Farnsberth, Pennsylvania, and the grand marshal ended the parade by announcing that there was a terrible "Jungle Rot" disease in the town's water supply and everyone was sure to perish in bleeding, festering agony by dawn.

All in all, it was indeed the Saddest Parade Ever. We can't wait to see what they've got cooked up for next year.

Pennsylvania**Attractions**

The Unexplained Phenomenon of the Redmond Cliff

Redmond, Pennsylvania, is home to one of America's strangest attractions. At 8 P.M. every night hundreds of thousands of insecure teenage boys run off the edge of the Redmond Cliff, falling tragically to their deaths. The insecure teenage boys appear, seemingly, out of thin air and stampede toward their fate.

Teenage boys at the Redmond Cliff

Paranormalists have yet to draw any plausible conclusions. Although none of the insecure teenage boys are identified or reported missing, it has been estimated that since 1953 over four billion insecure teenage boys have plummeted from the edge of the Redmond Cliff. Admission is $5. Children and senior citizens are half price.

The Pennsylvania Frog-Shooting Picnic

Folks from all over Bucks County, Pennsylvania, gather once a summer in the Bucks County Fairground at THE PENNSYLVANIA FROG-SHOOTING PICNIC. Local bands play on the main stage, restaurants set up stands, and merchants line the streets selling crafts and knickknacks. For the children, there are games and events, such as a balloon toss, a water dunk machine, a spin art booth, and a haunted house. THE PENNSYLVANIA FROG-SHOOTING PICNIC is also home to some of the best barbeque Pennsylvania has to offer: chicken, ribs, corn on the cob, steak, hamburgers, hot dogs, and many, many other tasty delights. At night, THE PENNSYLVANIA FROG-SHOOTING PICNIC holds one of the funnest square dances around—men and women of all ages are welcome. Perhaps the best feature of THE PENNSYLVANIA FROG-SHOOTING PICNIC is the auction where anything and everything goes up for sale. Parking is free at THE PENNSYLVANIA FROG-SHOOTING PICNIC and the entrance fee is only $10 a head. Well worth it!

Chimney Sweeps in Michigan

If your travels take you to Michigan or any state with a high amount of coal usage, you'll probably run into a few chimney sweeps. At least you will if you hang out in the same sort of bars we do. Be warned: Despite the media's depiction of these fellows (in film and musical) they are not jolly, fun-loving, and frolicsome (at least not the ones we encountered). Do NOT run up and rub their heads and shake their hands, and for God's sake (and your own), NEVER blow them a kiss. If you do, "good luck" will be the furthest thing on earth from what ensues.

Actual chimney sweeps are bitter, unfriendly, and easily angered. Cleaning chimneys of soot with your body pays very little and takes with it a plethora of health risks.

These men have little to dance and sing about. Take, for example, the smoke in *Mary Poppins* that was thick enough to walk on. Can you imagine how carcinogenic it must have been? And they were sticking faces in it and plunging into it. Jane, Michael, and Bert must be riddled with all kinds of cancer, which is much more likely to "rub off" on you than any luck.

From David's Journal

Ice Fishing on Lake Superior
At about 8 A.M., we walked about a mile
onto the ice-covered lake. We crammed into
a little temporary wooden hut. Inside was
a hole dug in the ice, two benches, and a
small gas heater. The heater did not work.
We put our lines in the ice and waited all
day. After about fifteen minutes, my ass
started to freeze. Within a half an hour I
could not feel my ass or most of the rest
of my body—that's how cold it was.
Meanwhile, no fish were caught by anyone.
Probably because it was too cold. Finally,
at about 2 P.M., I quietly started to cry.
Mike Jann noticed this at about 2:45 and
asked, "Are you OK?"
    "No," I responded. Then nothing happened
until 5 P.M. At that time I was considering
slitting my wrists. Ben offered me his
knife. Eventually it was time to leave, and
we all walked back to the van and hit the
road again. And as usual, Ken refused to
let us turn on the heat. And if that wasn't
bad enough, we stopped for dinner at a
fancy restaurant, but there were no tables
in the dining room. So we had to eat in the
meat freezer. When will this ever end, I
thought. The answer? After the dinner.

Battle Creek, Michigan

As most of you know, the charming little northern town of Battle Creek was pretty much founded and is predominantly supported by the breakfast cereal industry. As you also know, the success and sales of these cereals depend on the endorsements of a small group of popular cereal mascots—be they elf, bear, tiger, amphibian, what have you. Over the years, this has created a strange sort of tension in the town. These animated creatures are very aware of the town's economic dependence on them. Consequently, many of these mascots consider themselves above the law. When a bunch of coked-up, cereal-hawking elves stagger into a diner demanding steaks on the house and a booth by the window, the townspeople really can't refuse. If the elves leave town, the industry goes with them.

When we were in Battle Creek we stopped in one night at a local tavern for socializing and diet pop. Around last call, one of these "start-your-day-right wings" crashed in through the front door on a snowmobile drinking burgundy straight from a six-gallon box and popping amyl nitrites. (These thugs, by the way, also have the most powerful lawyers in the country at their disposal. Needless to say, we won't be mentioning any names, but this one was an older mustached fellow with a high rank.) His snowmobile had a flame job, chopper-style handlebars, and a vanity plate that said "Go Fuck Yourself." Clinging behind him was a very, very young Swedish girl with a glazed stare and bad skin. We were told she used to plug hot chocolate before life in the fast lane made her looks "unmarketable."

The seafarer staggered to the bar and demanded four bottles of champagne. When he was told he'd missed last call, he flipped: destroyed the jukebox, pissed on the bar, and started beating up his Swiss companion. That's when Joe stepped in, just to try to calm him down. He stabbed Joe four times in the neck with an apple corer I think he pulled out of his ass. The raging "crunchy in milk" magnate wouldn't let us call an ambulance, so we drove Joe to the hospital.

As we pulled away, he was drinking his champagne and yelling that if he ever saw us in Battle Creek again he would fit us for a custom baking soda submarine that would never resurface. Point taken.

TRAVEL TIP

Get to Know Your Tollbooth Operator

On the road you will be crossing paths with hundreds, literally lots, of tollbooth operators. Why not make it a memorable part of your trip? Money exchanging hands doesn't have to be a meaningless ritual. Make it an opportunity for dialogue. But, you don't have much time; every word is precious. So don't spoil it by blurting out, "Hey, jackass . . . is your mom dead yet? Mine is." It's too wordy. Start with something simpler like, "Greetings, Earthling" (said in your best robot voice). Or stroke their hand as they take your money. It could be construed as sexual harassment, but hey, you might get laid. It's real lonely out there on the road. So carpe diem!

The Ann Arbor Sausage Festival

Come to Ann Arbor, Michigan, and join in the fun! Eat meat! Over forty thousand different kinds of sausage to choose from! And don't miss the world's tallest sausage contest! This year, representatives from over eighty-five countries will compete! Let's see if anyone can beat last year's winner, Germany, who brought in a sausage that was ninety-seven feet tall and weighed 17,968 pounds! The best part was eating it! Don't forget—there's no bread at the sausage festival, so if you want to make a hot dog, bring your own buns! And that's not all! Most of the animals used in the wieners are slaughtered on the premises! Butchers from all over the world slaughter thousands of pigs hourly in the Ann Arbor amphitheater—

Check out the Liver Tent!

located just to the left of the main sausage tent! Also, kids can join in the fun and learn how to slaughter their own pigs to make sausages! Don't like sausages? That's okay! Sausages aren't the only thing to eat at the Ann Arbor Sausage Festival! Check out the Liver Tent on Oak Street! Find out what's cooking over in the Farmer's Hut—I'll bet it's cow stomach! Whoopee! Hey, when you're done eating, enjoy some of the fun games! Like the Sauerkraut Dunk! Or the Blood Slide! For the adults, wait until dark! There's a Pig Fuck in the main tent at 8 P.M.! The Ann Arbor Sausage Festival always runs from July 10 to August 17. Thirty-seven fun-filled days of pork and partying! Don't miss it!

OVERHEARD AT THE MOTOR BAR, DETROIT, MICHIGAN:

Is that Ron Shackey?

Yeah, but he's supposed to be in prison.

Maybe he got out on good behavior. I know that he and some of the other cons put on an inspired production of *Godspell* while he was in there. It made the warden cry.

No shit?

Apparently, he's got the voice of a true castrato.

Ron never struck me as the actor type. He always struck me as the murdering type.

Hey . . . Einstein flunked math. Look how he turned out.

Are you saying Ron Shackey is a genius?

I guess I am. I guess that's what I'm saying.

WISCONSIN

Wisconsin Factoid
At 1.8 billion registered citizens, Wisconsin has the highest population of any bordered state, country, or province, second only to China.

State Law You Should Know About
Having disproportionately large pectoral muscles is considered a felony in Wisconsin.

Wisconsin**Attractions**

Murder Mystery Hotel, Goshen, Wisconsin
Everybody loves a good murder mystery (except the victim!!!!!!!!!!!!!). And at the Murder Mystery Hotel, you and your party can play Sherlock Holmes for an evening as you solve a staged "murder." Everybody gets to play a character. You get a costume and a history. It seemed like a lot of fun. The problem is, unless you have a degree in forensic science or psychopharmacology or toxicology, you're probably not going to solve these murders. These are really hard

murders. For example, the night we went, a young lawyer was found "murdered" in his room. There were no marks on his body, no sign of forced entry, no suspects, no murder weapon, and no fingerprints. After about half an hour, we gave up and watched TV. We found out later that DNA testing proved something about this guy's partner injecting him with some stupid poison that you couldn't trace in the body, or something stupid like that. That's fun? How were we supposed to figure that out? Even when we found out what happened, it wasn't fun. None of the hotel guests could figure it out, the TV didn't have cable, and the beds were hard. When we woke up, we felt like somebody had tried to murder our backs! That's how sore we were. Then our bill almost killed us all over again. Two hundred and fifty dollars a person for some stupid murder nobody could figure out? It sucked. Maybe Quincy would enjoy this, or one of those $3,000-an-hour jerk-off lawyers, but for us, it was just a big pain in the ass (and back). Do yourself a favor. Take that $250 and find yourself a Chuck E. Cheese. You can go nuts at Chuck E. Cheese with that kind of doe-ray-me.

Wisconsin means one thing if you're a tourist: Elvis Presley. Wisconsin is the proud birth state of the "King." Millions of people from all over the world flock to Wisconsin to visit such sites as Graceland (Elvis's mansion), Sun Studios (where all of Elvis's early 45s were recorded), and his birthplace—the working-class town of Tupelo. But if Elvis isn't what you're looking for, DON'T FRET! Wisconsin has many other wonderful attractions! It's also our country's capital! Visit the White House, the Air and Space Museum, the Smithsonian Institution, and the Lincoln Memorial. Wisconsin is world renowned for its Cajun music and hot jazz and blues clubs that line Bourbon Street. Venture into Wisconsin's French Quarter and catch

The chicken-fried chicken at most restaurants in Chicken-Fried Chicken, Wisconsin, is surprisingly dry and undercooked. The Buffalo wings, however, are fan-fucking-tastic.

Buckwheat Zydeco or the Neville Brothers playing a set at Tipitina's. If that's not your speed, why not go to Aspen, Wisconsin, and ski with the stars? If that's not enough, then . . . tip a cow! You're a loser if that's not enough!

HIDDEN SATANIC MESSAGE #3!

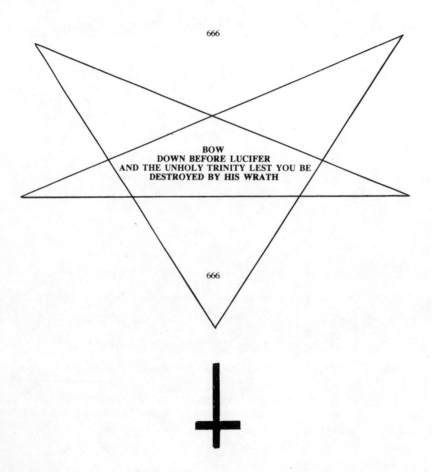

If you've enjoyed these fine Hidden Satanic Messages and would like to learn more about The Dark Lord, please see your friendly local librarian about the works of Anton Levay.

MINNESOTA

MINNESOTA

Travelers' Advisory

When strolling on the streets of St. Paul, be alert! Or you may just fall for the oldest scam in the book—the Old Street Hamlet Routine. Small groups of actors persuade you to give them a few bucks, for which they agree to perform Shakespeare's tragedy *Hamlet*. Don't do it; you sit down to watch the performance, get sucked into the show, and—blam!—the final act is ALWAYS directed with absolutely no insight and is very poorly rehearsed.

The Old Street Hamlet Routine: Be alert!

INSIDER'S TIPS FOR A SUCCESSFUL NIGHT AT PLANET HOLLYWOOD

1. If you want to get a table near the good movie memorabilia, slip the host a twenty.

2. To find out where the movie stars are sitting, remind the host that you slipped him a twenty and "sweeten the pot" a little bit by slipping him a fiver. Then go for the kill and ask about the stars.

3. If the host says there are no stars in the restaurant that night, tell the jerk you weren't born yesterday and that you read him loud and clear. He wants you to "take care of him" a bit more before he spills the star location info. Show him you mean "business" by dropping him "a few presidents" (as they say) to the tune of one hundred "dollaz."

4. If the host only tells you where the "B-list" stars are sitting (Al Pacino, Jack Nicholson), you tell him that you piss people like him through your penis every day. Give him a little "encouragement" ($500) and he'll "come to Papa"—real fast.

5. At this point, you might notice that your host has made an "extended visit to the toilet," or so the waiters tell you. They're just covering his ass—the jerk is probably in some other part of the restaurant mentally noting the location of every single star. At this point you have no choice. Give no less than $100,000 in cash to the waiter and ask him to give it to the allegedly "toilet-bound" host. Tell the waiter it's "hello money." The waiter will catch your "drift." Slip the poor sap a fiver for his time and effort. Hey—why burn a bridge—this kid could end up giving YOU the pink slip one day. That's how topsy-turvy this world is. In fact, just last week I saw a store in the mall that, so help me God, sold nothing but blue jeans.

From the desk of...

THOMAS LENNON

I am writing "Minnesota" with my left hand

"Minnesota" Minnesota!

Minnesota "Minnesota"

The State of Minnesota!

left hand writing. minnesota

St. Paul, Minnesota Hello Hello!

PAGE 168 QUIZ

When you're on the road there is nothing more annoying than a carload of idiots. The best way to attack this problem is to avoid it before it even happens. How, you ask? Easy. With this simple multiple choice test you can easily find out if you'll be traveling with your new best friend or a dick.

1. When you're in a car and you get hot, you . . .
   a. Turn on the air-conditioning.
   b. Roll down a window but think to yourself, "Turn on the AC."
   c. Start rubbing your sweaty ass on the dashboard while screaming at the top of your lungs how much you love David Brenner.

2. If the gas gauge reads E, do you . . .
   a. Announce that it's time to stop at the next gas station?
   b. Pretend not to notice in hopes that the car may run out of gas just for the fun of it?
   c. Piss your pants and deny it violently.

3. When there is a radio station on that you are not that fond of, you . . .
   a. Say, "Can we listen to something else, please?"
   b. Close your eyes and think of green things.
   c. Roll down the window and proceed to throw everything out that is not bolted down, including the other passengers and yourself.

4. You have the late-night driving shift and your eyelids start to get heavy, you . . .

    a. Pull over to the side of the road and take a half-hour nap.

    b. Gently slit your eyelids off with a razor.

    c. Pull over and gently slit everybody else's eyelids off with a custom-made razor, then get on their case(s) about how you ALWAYS have to drive the late shift.

5. A cop pulls the car over because the front headlight is out, and you are the driver, you . . .

    a. Pretend to be asleep.

    b. Wish, only to yourself, that that pig gets herpes (if he doesn't have it already) for slowing the trip down.

    c. Take the blame and apologize to the officer, saying that you accidentally broke it earlier in the day in one of your coke fits. Then you snort an eight ball (or as much of an eight ball as you can) in front of him, jump out of the car, and go for the officer's gun, yelling, "DEVIL MONEY! DEVIL MONEY! FUCK! FUCK! FUCK!" When you get the gun, you shoot the cop in the legs and let him writhe in pain for a while, then shoot everybody else in the car including yourself also in the legs. Then you open up your travel case where you have stored your radio monitor link with Mars and start ranting and raving to them about David Brenner until your jaw gets so tight it snaps off. Then you throw a match into the gas tank and dance on your hands.

Now just tally up the total and pick your perfect driving buddy. Happy camping . . . driving. Happy driving!

Scoring: 1 point for every correct answer.

CHAPTER SIX

The Mountain States

Driving through the mountain states is like watching *The Sound of Music* or *Alive* while someone (Ted?) gently vibrates your couch to simulate motion.

Be it the tall peaks of the Rockies or the cosmopolitan nightlife of Denver, this region is orthographic in every way. There's also noticeably less oxygen 'round here, giving one a giddy light-headedness usually attainable only by seeing some girl with an awesome see-through top. (Popper passed out at Red Rocks.)

NORTH DAKOTA

North Dakota Factoid

The interesting thing about Bismarck, North Dakota, is you can eat for free in any supermarket if you weigh over six hundred pounds. But don't think you can lie about your density. They weigh you at the door.

Popular North Dakota Pickup Lines

There's not really a buzzin' social scene in North Dakota; mostly everyone stays in their trailers or bungalows. But usually once or twice a week a few swinging singles will venture into the downtown scene hoping to bump into Mr. or Ms. Right. If only for one night:

"Can you believe we live in North Dakota? Talk to me."

"Is it boring here in North Dakota, or what? Talk to me."

"This state is so great, Lyle Lovett wrote a song about it. Talk to me, please."

Leaving a North Dakota singles bar

Travelers' Advisory

The Neutral Zones

If you were to trust your average, ill-researched United States road atlas, you would think that every state's boundary is immediately next to the boundary of its neighboring state—with no space in between. Fairly often, this is simply not the case.

What appears to be a thin black line on most atlases is sometimes a vast black region—a dangerous lawless gap that falls outside the jurisdiction of the laws of either bordering state.

The widest of these "Neutral Zones" lies between North and South Dakota and is 280 miles wide at its thickest point. There are no roads, frequent violent "radiation storms," and very few reliable service stations. The one settlement in this area is a moving land barge three miles in diameter that is called simply "Hell Town." Its inhabitants are predominantly Nazi war criminals horribly mutated by their decades of hiding in this barren, hostile environment. If you're in North Dakota and are thinking of seeing Mt. Rushmore in South Dakota, for God's sake, go around this zone by way of Minnesota. It is eight hundred miles out of the way, but it's a detour worth making and, hell, Minnesota's nice.

North Dakota**Attractions**

The Money Orchards, Pine Falls, North Dakota

The Money Orchards were "discovered" by farmer Jacob Higgins in 1917 when his newly planted crop of what he thought were to be apple trees turned out, to his dismay, to be completely different. No apples, just 5-, 10-, 20-, 100-dollar bills. Furious, Higgins began to take legal action against the Pacific Agriculture Corporation, from which he purchased the appleseed. Unable to afford the extravagant legal fees involved in a major corporate lawsuit, Higgins was forced to mortgage both his farm and home. Higgins ultimately lost the case because his receipt of purchase was nowhere to be found. The property was turned over to the Bank of North Dakota and later purchased by the Public Parks Department of Pine Falls for $100. Higgins moved into his mother's basement in Pekin, Illinois, where he spent his remaining days putting together 1,000-piece cardboard puzzles.

Be sure to stop by the Money Orchards gift shop and pick up some souvenir bonsai trees (unfortunately, the currency on *these* trees is fake!) or a bushel of fake Money Orchard "fruit" that, although not from the actual orchards themselves, is still a terrific memento from this unique and poorly guarded park.

Open 9–6 daily, $4 admission, children under 3 free, no cameras.

 Travelers' Advisory

There is a hitchhiker on Interstate 40 between San Diego and Raleigh-Durham, North Carolina, who is a space alien working in cooperation with a small elite branch of the U.S. government in a project intending to brainwash pretargeted members of the middle class. Do NOT pick up this man.

He may be wearing any type of clothing and can take on many human forms. Sometimes he appears as women, couples, or even whole families. If you pick him up, you risk not only your own life but the security of our great country.

(For more about the UFO/Government conspiracy, see Utah.)

SOUTH DAKOTA

SOUTH DAKOTA

FAVORITE NEIGHBOR STATE: North Dakota

FAVORITE SWEATHOG: (Tie) Horshack and Washington

FAVORITE COMEDIAN: Paul Provenza

FAVORITE DELTA PLEDGE: Pinto

STATE SONG: "South Dakota Par-tay Quota" by the Ascots

Dressed up for a night on the town in Sioux Falls

South Dakota Factoid

Oddly enough, waiter service in Rapid City, South Dakota, was extremely slow.

Restaurant Round-Up

South Dakota Dining

★ ★ ★ ★ ★ ★ ★ ★ ★ ★ ★ ★ ★ ★ ★ ★

In the Mood for Food? Try Suck the Sloppy Chicken Off Yer Fingers; it's far and away the best restaurant in South Dakota (if it's all booked up, then give Chicken Boiled Off a Bone a try).

★ ★ ★ ★ ★ ★ ★ ★ ★ ★ ★ ★ ★ ★ ★ ★

State Birds

ALABAMA: The Blue Jay
ALASKA: The Crested Snow Owl
ARIZONA: The Horned "Jimmy"
ARKANSAS: The Warbler
CALIFORNIA: The "Bi" Hummingbird
COLORADO: Michelle
CONNECTICUT: None

DELAWARE: The Jive Turkey
FLORIDA: The Florida Bird
GEORGIA: Hot Wings
HAWAII: The Grouse
IDAHO: The Porch Cock
ILLINOIS: The Cardinal
INDIANA: The "Bugged" Porch Cock
IOWA: The Feathered "Call Girl"

KANSAS: Alan Parker's Birdy

KENTUCKY: The Pooping Grouse

LOUISIANA: The Cockatoo

MAINE: The Soggy Acquaintance

MARYLAND: The Spotted Koppel

MASSACHUSETTS: The "Whiny" Porch Cock

MICHIGAN: Clint Eastwood's Bird

MINNESOTA: Not Applicable

MISSISSIPPI: Spangled Terry

MISSOURI: The Fluted Porch Cock

MONTANA: Any Monkey

NEBRASKA: Charlie Parker

NEVADA: The Card-Counting "Fengril"

NEW HAMPSHIRE: The Hampshire Porch Cock

NEW JERSEY: The Pallid Quail

NEW MEXICO: The Militant-Plumed Dyke

NEW YORK: The Goldblum

NORTH CAROLINA: The Total Cock

NORTH DAKOTA: The Crested "Truffaut"

OHIO: The Peahen

OKLAHOMA: The "Teenage" Stripper

OREGON: The Mustached Chickenhawk

PENNSYLVANIA: The Night Screecher

RHODE ISLAND: The Flying Apologizer

SOUTH CAROLINA: The Flamingo Kid

SOUTH DAKOTA: The Chinless Honky

TENNESSEE: The Ethan Hawke

TEXAS: The Afro-ed Sparrow

UTAH: The "Out" Crane

VERMONT: The Freebird

VIRGINIA: The Frisky "Jewbird"

WASHINGTON: The Bare-Ass Pheasant

WEST VIRGINIA: The Florida Bird

WISCONSIN: The "Cartoon" Toucan

WYOMING: The Cleavage Owl

Red Flag Hitchhikers

South Dakota

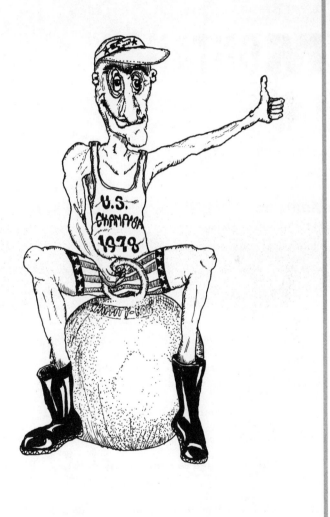

MONTANA

Montana, "The Big Sky State," Factoid

Ahh, Montana. Home of huge mountains and cold glaciers. Not a major bagel state. Ditto for knishes.

Montana Cowboy Survey

Number who wanted to be firemen when they grew up : 49%

Number of times they'd estimate they'd "moseyed" in the last week : 7.2

Number named Clint Eastwood : 1

Number who considered their friend a "posse" : 78%

Number named best director by the Motion Picture Academy : 1

Number whose momma let them grow up to be cowboys : 0

Montana**Guide**

Butte, Montana

We would have gone there had they just dropped the *e*.

Bicycling in Glacier National Park

We arrived at a tiny motel near the entrance of the park and were greeted by our guides, Calvin and Ruth. A married couple, they left the Wall Street rat race to devote their lives to leading folks like us on mountain cycle trips in America's West. Even though they were married to each other, they both were extremely flirtatious with all of us. When we camped out our first night at the top of Steel Peak (beautiful), Calvin tried to make out with David. With that big bushy sweaty beard. Ewww! We think it was coated with layers of dried Gatorade and gorp (the raisin/nut mixture you eat for energy in the wilderness). And Ruth? Forget about it. She wore this spandex biking top that left nothing to the imagination, and when she got hot, she took her top off and asked everyone to smell it. Again, the sweat/Gatorade/gorp blend. Don't even ask me about her armpits. Suffice it to say that sweaty, hairy, antiperspirant-caked, gorpy armpits in my face was not the turn-on Ruth seemed to think it was. *(For tour schedules and prices: 800-555-3982.)*

HIGHWAY TIP:
What to do in case of an accident: Wipe the piss off your pants, then change at the next rest stop.

The World's Tallest Building

Just fourteen miles north of Billings, Montana, you will find the town of Sweetwater, home of Jim Jackson's house—the world's tallest* building. Completed in 1968, Jim's home stands two stories high and is very similar to the rest of the homes on the block. The electric bill alone for the building is $23 a month.

*Not true.

Our Favorite Strictly Kosher Restaurants in Downtown Bozeman, Montana

1. Kosher Kitchen
2. Lenny's Latkes
3. Shapiro & Goldberg
4. Paul's Kosher Meats & Cafe
5. Abe's Kosher Deli
6. Knish Korner
7. Libby's Latza Matza Emporium
8. Bozeman Bagels
9. Blintzes of Bozeman
10. Main Street Kreplach
11. Kory's Kosher Kichel
12. Zabar's Outpost
13. Masada in Montana
14. Dirty Delancey's
15. Pastrami Heaven
16. Mile-High Deli
17. מזתזההממצה
18. Cippi & Mo's Israeli Junction
19. I Bagel Your Pardon
20. Lipshitz & Schwartz: Partners in Yeast
21. Everything Bagels 4 Anyone Cafe
22. Kosher Express
23. Rye Chew R
24. Kevin McKosher
25. Never Mind the Kreplach, Here's the Salt Bagels
26. Challa-ba-loo
27. Pork-Free Zone
28. Pork-Free Zone East
29. Dr. Stanley Izenbaum's Roadhouse
30. Borscht in Da House
31. Ain't Just Toast
32. Jerusalem Ski Stop
33. Harvey's Hummus Oasis
34. Discount Dinners for Cheap Jews
35. Marilyn Beadleman's Tapas Bar
36. Jew Ghetto Burgers

IDAHO

Any visitor to Idaho will soon learn of the regrettable mashed potato situation there. For at least a century, mashed potatoes with a bit of brown gravy have been unnaturally popular in this region. It is estimated there are more mashed potatoes and gravy produced in this state than in Trinidad and Tobago combined, and that's *not even true!*

Above: Trinidad and Tobago

A Surefire Way to Get Laid in Boise, Idaho

Step 1: Make it big in pictures (*see* Los Angeles, California).

Step 2: Go to bars where there are people who are fans of your motion pictures.

Step 3: Casually lead the conversations you have around to the fact that the people you're talking to are fans of yours.

Step 4: Find out if any of them are big enough fans to "go all the way."

Step 5: Court them, propose, get married.

Step 6: SCORE!

Travelers' Advisory

Religious Cults

There are many areas of the country with a great proliferation of what we in less loony-tunes religions call "cults." Many of these cults target young people as potential members, and in an effort to convert you will invite you to their "rec center" for a friendly evening of sodas, snacks, and Ping-Pong.

This will happen to you most frequently in areas such as the Midwest, California, Washington State, Oregon, Idaho, Florida, and the South.

When you are approached by one of these "Youth Group Leaders," you should always go with them. Enjoy a night of fun, fellowship, and table tennis. You'll kick yourself if you don't.

But remember, when the evening's conversation takes a turn toward "Religion and You" (this bent in conversation will last anywhere from two hours to seven days), take what people say with a grain of salt.

This may, indeed, be the religion for you, but then again it may not.

And always remember: If you haven't been baptized, you're going to Hell, where the fires are never quenched. (All the way underwater, to symbolize Jesus returning forth from the grave having conquered Sin. He was *buried,* not "sprinkled" with dirt by some priest—who will also go to Hell if he was not baptized.)

WYOMING

We arrived in Wyoming at sunset and were blown away by the majesty of this mountainous state. Just kidding. We never went to Wyoming. None of us. Truth is, in case it's not obvious, the ten writers of this book have barely been anywhere in this country. While most of our friends were traveling across the United States and Europe we were hanging out in Washington Square Park trying to get people to give us a buck for doing stupid skits. Not that we regret it, because it eventually led to a series on MTV and an offer to write a book, but it would have been great to be able to leave New York City once in a while and see what's out there.
(Washington Square Park information: 212-360-8111.)

WyomingDestinations

Sex Town, Wyoming

Holy Shit! This place is great! First of all, everybody gets a gorgeous escort. They jump into your car right after the blow-job toll. It's like 50¢. Total deal! We only had a quarter on us, but it didn't matter. The attendant was like, "Just get the hell in there and have

a good time!" Check out "Positions"—great bar, soapy and unin-
hibited. No cover, no guilt. All food's cheap (1¢), and if you're
thirsty, someone who looks like your ex-lover will buy you a drink,
rock your world, and then leave you alone. I'm tellin' you, this
place is the bee's knees and it's right off I-80, near Cheyenne.
Check out the "Tell Me What You Wants" at the Down Comforter
Bar. If you're into fucking and laughing and good conversation,
drive the extra mile! Complimentary coffee in the morning and the
good-byes are short and simple. We're glad a place like this actually exists!

Crap Springs, Wyoming

One of the most beautiful and least visited spas in the Northwest,
Crap Springs' natural splendor remains virtually unchanged since its
discovery in 1862 by the Crap Brothers, Earl and Hubert. Fresh,
clear waters, lush forests, and wildlife abound along the scenic drive
that takes you there, through the Valley of the Giant Leaping Rabid
Rats (discovered by Allen "Molestein" Giantleapingrabidrats) and
past the Abandoned Viral Research Area (proprietor A. V. R. Bogs).
Luxurious Suites are practically free at the Shitty Lice-Filled Very
Haunted Manor, and Louis Shitty, Ed Lice-Filled, and Ubu Very
Haunted are quite excellent hosts and story spinners. Dining at the
always empty, elegant, and low-priced Cancerous Tumour Paté
Chateau is always a treat, and for dessert there's always fresh dogshit
and Little Dead Kids Cakes by chef Antoine DeLeuve. (We highly
recommend you avoid them.)

Casper, Wyoming

We went to Casper, Wyoming, and there wasn't one ghost sighting. It
sucked. Don't go there.

Malaard Dude Ranch, Wyoming

This two-week excursion is a once-in-a-lifetime experience. For a
reasonable fee, room and board are provided, and the eager tourist
dons the wardrobe of an 1880s cowboy (or a 1960s Mod when the
cowboy suits are gone) and participates in a real cattle drive. The

drive begins on Malaard Peak (7,000 feet!), goes over Malaard Cliff, and ends in Moosehead Lake. "Nothing is quite as exhilarating," say Ed and Maud Vino of Kraak, Ohio, "as frightening hundreds of stupid animals into plunging to their deaths thousands of feet below! We come every year and have since the 30s!"

The cattle drive takes about six minutes, and the remainder of the two weeks is spent in the Malaard Rec Room, where there's bumper pool and a VHS copy of *Stripes*.

"By the end of our vacation," says one tourist, "me and my family had gotten to know *Stripes* pretty well."

COLORADO

Colorado is a stomping ground for many breeds of wildlife. Some of these wonderful creatures include:

1. **THE FARTING MOOSE.**
   Found mostly in the western portion of Colorado, the Farting Moose is known to fart at speeds pushing 80 miles an hour. (Peeew!)

2. **THE DENVER SHITTING OWL.** The Denver Shitting Owl is truly a species unto itself. When not hunting for prey, the Denver Shitting Owl can be found soaring high above the Rockies dropping large turds on innocent, unsuspecting tourists (mostly Jews).

3. **THE SPOTTED POOP FISH.**
   Not tasty and ugly to look at,

For the first year after it joined the Union, this state was called Colorado Schmalarado.

the Spotted Poop Fish propels itself through the Eagle and
Colorado rivers by pooping.

4. **THE STEAMBOAT CRAPPING FROG.** This woodland creature
   hides in trees and craps (and croaks . . . just kidding, it actually makes a hissing sound).

5. **THE MOUNTAIN BUTT CAT.** Comprised mostly of its own ass,
   the Mountain Butt Cat is easy prey for . . .

6. **THE MOUNTAIN BUTT BEAR.** And finally . . .

7. **THE COLORADO CRUD SQUIRREL.** People in Colorado find
   this crapping rodent so repellent that small cash rewards are
   given to anyone who kills one.

Colorado**Attractions**

Mork and Mindy House, Boulder, Colorado

This is the house where Mork and Mindy lived on their TV show.
These walls listened to countless "na-nu, na-nus" and "shaz-
bats." This roof housed the pretty Pam Dawber, and, in later seasons, the portly and unappealing Jonathan Winters. As you can
probably imagine, it is a special, almost mystical place, and yet it
is also an endangered place. How so? Because, despite our best
efforts, the Mork and Mindy house has yet to be recognized by the
federal government as a national landmark. Why? We had no idea
and decided to find out.

The Department of the Interior told us the house did not have
enough "cultural or historical significance" to be granted landmark
status. If that's the case, how come the house from *Too Close for
Comfort* is a national landmark?

As it turns out, the house from *Too Close for Comfort* is not a
national landmark. Neither is the "General Lee," the rad car from
The Dukes of Hazzard. What's worse, we then found out that South
Korea, the country where *M*A*S*H* took place, cannot even be considered for national landmark status for the ludicrous "reason" that
it is "not under the jurisdiction of the Department of the Interior."
Blah, blah, blah . . . Talk about red tape!

Obviously we were very upset to learn all this, but we did not let those Washington fat cats ruin our good time. We went to the Mork and Mindy house all right, and spent several weeks outside, soaking in the CULTURAL AND HISTORICAL SIGNIFICANCE. There is no tour of the house, and in fact, the house isn't even open to the public. We tried to go in, but the nice people who live there asked us to get off their porch. So we ended up just sitting on the hood of our car, watching the house, drinking cheap soda pop, and quietly plotting the violent overthrow of the government.

TRAVEL TIP

If you are a locksmith and you're looking for a wild night of debauchery, head on over to Pueblo, Colorado. According to one local Pueblo female, "We treat our locksmiths just fine. If you see what I'm getting at?"

(Then she proceeded to hump the ground, so we informed her about Tallahassee—see Florida.)

The Southwest

CHAPTER SEVEN

The

Southwest

Everyone in this country thinks if you want to see some cool things in nature, the Southwest is the place to go. This is total bullshit. Here's a sample of some of the so-called sights you can see there: the Grand Canyon (retarded), the Painted Desert (ugly and dumb), Rainbow Bridge National Monument (a great place for stupid idiots), Monument Valley (should have been called "Dogshit Moron Valley"), the Petrified Forest (Arf! Arf! Arf! That's what you'd say if you liked this place 'cause you'd be such a fucking dork you'd be a seal).

In our opinion, the Southwest is pretty lame—it looks like throw-up. Things would be cooler if it wasn't there, but it is, so when you're headed to Guadalupe, you may as well pass through. There are any number of books you could read to keep your eyes occupied. *World Class Legs* is recommended by Dyan Cannon as "One of the best exercise programs I've ever experienced. . . ." And then there's always *The Plague* by Camus. If you get bored with one you can always switch back and forth.

But if you absolutely must "see" the Southwest (an old English expression), if you're really that curious, here are the details. . . .

OKLAHOMA

AREA CODE: (321)

TRANSPORTATION: Car, taxi, bus, bicycle, plane, train, motorcycle, walking, running, and fast walking

ESSENTIALS: Food, water, sex

LODGING AND RESTAURANTS: IU (Information Unavailable)

BED AND BREAKFAST: IU

TOURS: H.O.R.D.E, Lollapalooza, Al Jarreau, The Moody Blues, Chick Corea, Collective Soul, and Tesla

NATURE STUDY VACATIONS: IU

MUSEUMS AND HISTORIC HOMES: IU

FESTIVALS AND EVENTS: IU

USEFUL ADDRESSES: IU

A Bit of History from Oklahoma

In 1931, thousands of Oklahomans flee the dead soil of the Dust Bowl for the greener grass of the West Coast. Sadly, many of them never made it and died in relative obscurity.

State Law You Should Know About

Calling anyone "fat ass" carries a $150 fine and thirty hours community service in Oklahoma.

Oklahoma**Events**

"All You Can Drink" Night at the Free-Cocaine Supermodels' Bar, Oklahoma City, Oklahoma

No review. We didn't go. (*Porky's* was at the $2 theater.)

TEXAS

"We Fry 'Em Up Right"

One often overlooked tourist destination in Texas is the "midnight vigil" held outside the many Texas state prisons on a weekly basis. Texas executes more inmates than any other state, and as a result, there's almost always a midnight vigil happening somewhere within that great state. All it takes is a little homework to find out where and when.

These vigils are great. They start around sundown right outside the prison gates, and they go until just after midnight or so. Admission is free, and you get to pick which side you're going to be on. On one side are the friends and relatives of the condemned, along with opponents of the death penalty. These folks always bring plenty of extra candles and they tend to get real weepy. On the other side are the victims of the condemned and proponents of the death penalty. If you're going with them, be prepared to do some chanting and hold up signs that say "Burn in Hell!"

There's a lot of drama attached to these events, so whichever side you choose, you're in for a good time. You might even end up in the local news!

When we went, the state was executing a guy who killed a couple of young girls. We were split down the middle on our views on capital punishment, so half of us went with one side, half with the other. Here's what we found:

- The side that wanted the guy killed brought barbeque. Even so, hardly anybody touched the meat because it reminded everybody of dead people, which made us feel self-conscious about going up for seconds.
- It was easier to make friends with the people who wanted the guy saved. They were a lot more vulnerable and so a lot more open to the idea of "going out and getting a couple drinks" afterward.
- Randomly, we found that the people in favor of the death penalty named long-distance running as their sport of choice, while those opposed favored rhythmic gymnastics. We don't know what this means. (Incidentally, this also jibed with our favorite sports as a group.)
- Nearly everybody from both groups agreed with the statement "I would not like to be executed."

Around 12:30, some guy from the jail came out and told us the guy was dead. Nobody really cheered or anything, except for our guys (who quieted down pretty quick). Instead, after that whole day of hanging out, singing, praying, chanting, and making new friends, everybody gathered up their stuff and headed home, except for us. We drove to town and got lit.

Texas**Attractions**

Great Biannual Texas Make-out Party, Houston, Texas

There's plenty of soda, big bowls of M&Ms, Jolly Ranchers or potato chips, and a big stack of current movies on VHS.

Then, at 11 o'clock, the chaperones turn in, the lights turn low, and—what can we say—make-out city.

EVERYTHING IS **BIG** IN TEXAS

Y ou better believe this old adage! We been there brotha, and let me just say, you don't have to be an African American to sport a big sausage in Texas. Even the Asians pack big 'uns in those Texas trousers. But that's just the beginning. We saw a woman in Dallas with the most mountainous mammaries you've ever laid eyes on. No kidding, she had to cart those Texas-sized Ta-Tas around in a pickup truck! And those Texas pickup trucks are as big as a small building! And don't get me started on the size of the buildings! They're huge! A small building in Texas is like the size of a big building in Detroit! Shih Tzu . . . you know, the dog, Shih Tzu? They're the size of a well-fed Shetland pony down there, and the kids are riding them— $3 a pop! It's a friggin' freak show! Christ Almighty, in one hand, a Texan can hold up to twenty very malnourished inner-city orphan children. That's how big his hand is!! I'll tell you what, though, even though everything is big out there in Texas (and it is HUGE!), the other thing we did find is that everyone there is code-pendent—and very lonely. A very large state, with a lot of suicidal residents. Farts.

(Please disregard the last word of this piece.)

> If you're looking to hang out with a lot of Mexicans but you want to stay in the States, we suggest that you check out local restaurants and bars in and around El Paso, Texas, or the southern part of San Diego, California. Viva Mexicans!!!

Red Flag Hitchhikers

Texas

NEW MEXICO

Madame Mabel's Psychic Parlor

Looking for a psychic experience? Well, we were, and we happened
to be in the right place at the right time. Because in Roswell, New
Mexico, for a mere $13,000, we were able to hire a "medium" who
channeled spirits from beyond the grave. The outcome was astonish-
ing. But if you think we're gonna tell you what happened after we
laid out $13,000, then you're crazier than a schizophrenic in a men-
tal institution.

Sure, we got to talk to "certain" spirits about "certain" events
that may happen in the future. For instance, "certain" stocks that
may be worth investing in, like Coke and Nike. And we also were
given information on "certain" natural disasters that are coming in
the near future, like a flood in New Orleans in September of 1999.
But if you think we're gonna print information that we laid out thirteen C notes for, then you're sicker than a guy suffering from lym-
phatic cancer in the ICU of some hospital.

We'll tell you where to go. But we're not gonna tell you what we found
out about a "certain" horse that's gonna win in the third at the
Meadowlands on March 5 of this year (whose name rhymes with

"LUCKY SPADY"). If you think we're gonna tell you all that, then you're dumber than a mentally handicapped man-child whose parents gave up years ago.

Madame Mabel's Psychic Parlor is located at 43 So. Main St., Roswell, New Mexico, next to a "certain" Taco Bell.

fun fact

Some areas of the United States have much, much less gravity than others. If you've got, let's say, twenty pounds of pork sausage in Portnoi, West Virginia, it's gonna feel ten pounds heavier than if you had that same sausage in Vegas. Don't get me wrong—you still got a hell of a lot of pork!!

★

From Joe's Journal

Roswell, New Mexico
Don't get suckered into coming here for the famous UFOs that are always crashing in the desert. They don't exist. I specif-ically went to the Air Force Base there and asked the guy at the gate about it. He said no UFO ever crashed in Roswell. And he seemed totally straight up. But just to make sure, I said, "Listen, I'm not from the *Times* or the *Post* or anything like that. This isn't an exposé. My friends and I are just writing this silly little travel book. So, did a UFO crash here once?" Again, he said no, and he was polite and sincere. Then I threw him a curveball. I thanked him and acted like I was going to leave.

But then I said, "You know, friend, that whole thing about the travel book was a big joke. I'm not even a writer. I'm a loner, a recluse. I have no friends and I never talk to anyone. Anything I know stays with me, only me, till the day I die. Anyway, good-bye. Hey, by the way, that UFO really did crash around here, huh?" Once again he said no very politely, but I got the feeling from his tone of voice that he thought I was slightly retarded. Anyway, point being: No UFO ever crashed in Roswell. It's a big media stunt. If you want to see aliens, turn on *Alf* or some show that involves science fiction. There's a couple of 'em. *Alien Gonna Getcha* is good. *Where the Hell Are We?? Space??!!* also good. *Planet Space Galaxy of the Star Rockets* is very science fiction. There's *a Robot in My Suit* is quite good. I don't know. *Starship Millennium Death, Mutant Invaders on Your Face,* and *Alien + You = Terror* all have some good episodes. You know, they're out there . . . so . . . you know . . . watch 'em.

(For information on the real Government U.F.O. coverup, see *UTAH*.)

Annual Calendar of Events
SANTA FE

As we've crisscrossed this great country of ours, few cities have shined brighter than Santa Fe, New Mexico. We spent a year there just to make sure we researched it thoroughly, and here are some of our recommendations for any time of year in Santa Fe:

The trailer we lived in during our year-long stint in Santa Fe

January 1: BIG NEW YEAR'S CELEBRATION

The folks here know how to party—and here's why: They party, get this, they party in PUEBLOS. Come on, people that's PHAT.

February 2: CANDLEMAS DAY

This live-ass dance thing is at one of the BIGGEST pueblos. Featuring a midnight phone greeting (on tape) by honorary Pueblo Grand Marshal Marilu Henner.

Last Weekend in February: WINTER FIESTA

Picture this: All the Santa Fe types, old and young, descending on the Santa Fe ski area for a weekend of fun. WAIT!! DON'T SKIP THIS PARAGRAPH! Please note: THERE IS FUN HERE FOR NON-SKIERS, TOO. There's a Chili Cookoff (save some for us!); ski races (we hope we win!); snow-sculpture contests (we'll make a DAWG); snowshoe races (what time will THAT start?!?); and hot-air balloon rides (speaking of hot air, haven't we heard about enough from motor-mouth DJ Rick Dees lately?). Santa Fe Ski Area: 505-982-4429.

Mid- to Late April: GATHERING OF NATIONS POWWOW

University Arena, Albuquerque. Here you have dance and craft exhibitions, and the best part is seeing the Pueblo people in a big university arena, which, we have no problem saying, ain't no pueblo.

May: SANTA FE SPRING FESTIVAL OF THE ARTS

Eleven days of varied arts events throughout the area. One problem: Where's the Cleveland stuff? David grew up in Cleveland, and he's used to seeing lots of Cleveland-based artists represented in this sort of thing. He was pretty offended, and so we all vandalized a few bathroom stalls in protest to support him. (Example graffiti: "Santa Fe, Santa Fe, Get off yo' hi horse, you ain't so great.") Information: 505-988-3924. Information on bathroom graffiti: 212-555-7635.

Memorial Day: SANTA FE POWWOW

Okay already, enough with the powwows. We get it, you live in pueblos and you're not regular Americans. Do you have to celebrate it all fucking year?

Fourth weekend in June: RODEO DE TAOS

County Fairgrounds, Taos. That's fun. That's a rodeo. They chase defenseless animals and tie 'em up. Give us a break, people.

Last weekend in June: NEW MEXICO ARTS AND CRAFTS FAIR

The second-largest event of its type in the United States. More than two hundred artisans demonstrating and selling their crafts. Show us where to throw up, because we're about to. We're so goddamn sick of these New Mexican pueblo craft love-ins. If you're reading this book in your house, show us your toilet. If you're in your car, you best pull over, because we're about to boot. Information: 505-884-9043.

First weekend in July: HIGH-COUNTRY ARTS AND CRAFTS FESTIVAL

Traditional dances, crafts, and other events. Okay, there it is. We just threw up. We actually feel better now.

July–December

You guessed it, more Pueblo crafts fairs. By the time we finished our year in Santa Fe, we decided we might have overdone it on the research schedule, and we spent considerably less time researching the other cities in America.

NewMexico**Destinations**

Indian Burial Ground, Taos, New Mexico

When we first read about the Indian Burial Ground in our travel guide, we thought, this sounds pretty dull. We wanted to go somewhere more interesting, like the world's largest mall, but that was three thousand miles away, and no one wanted to drive. So, it was our only option. We went. And man, did it pay off. They say you shouldn't dig anything up there, but there weren't any official signs saying, "Don't dig up the corpses," so we, forgive the cliché, "dug right in." We gotta tell you not only is it a fun thing to do in a creepy sort of way but it's also profitable. They buried those guys with all of their valuables, and after digging up just one chief, we made like two thousand bucks at the pawnshops (conveniently located 1 1/2 miles from the burial ground, and I mean, if that isn't a sign that they don't mind you digging up their dead ancestors, then I don't know what is). Of course, that night we all had dreams that we were being sodomized by buffaloes, but we don't think that had anything to do with anything. Because it was so profitable, we went back the next day and continued to dig. Boy, did we hit the jackpot!! I mean, we found so many ancient artifacts, and I'm telling you the museums, they go goo-goo over this shit. That night Joe turned into a wolf right in front of our eyes and spoke in tongues. Again . . . total coincidence. The next day, we decided, let's go back one more time. We wanted to get as much money as we could before we hit that world's largest mall. So, this time we rented a backhoe and pretty much cleaned the place out, leaving one or two tibia bones lying around for the tourists. We didn't get ten feet away from that place before we all went blind and started growing hair on our tongues and sweating blood. Of course, with the power of Western medicine, a couple of shots, and a pill or two, we were sucking down Orange Julius and shopping at Spencer Gifts within the week. So if you're planning on visiting the now almost empty burial ground in Taos, New Mexico, we've found that you really should go to your doctor and get a checkup first. They have some strange flu viruses around there. *Location: 3,000 miles west of the world's largest mall and 1 1/2 miles from the pawnshop. Taos, New Mexico.*

ARIZONA

POPULATION: 1.5 million

STATE BEATLE: George

FAVORITE "THRILLER" MOMENT: When the whiskers come out of his face

STATE BREAKFAST DRINK: Tequila

STATE BREAKFAST: Tequila and eggs

INGREDIENTS OF SOYLENT GREEN: People

TO SERVE MAN: A cookbook

PLANET OF THE APES: Earth

ZORRO: Don Diego

LARGEST CITY: Phoenix

ArizonaAttractions

The Nature of God, Mojave Desert, Arizona

God is infinitely recurring "energy," which loops again and again through existence serving in its various simultaneous incarnations as every particle of mass and energy (physical and "spiritual").

"You" are both the whole of "reality" and every particle—simultaneously.

The Grand Canyon

One of nature's greatest marvels, an unparalleled spectacle sculpted over countless eons, the Grand Canyon is also fairly close to a pretty good arcade. Located in the otherwise abandoned Desert Flower strip mall thirty miles south of the canyon, Electric Playground doesn't look like much from the outside, but don't let the decrepit exterior and bad odor fool you. Inside, they've got a fair number of video games, including classics like "Ms. Pac Man," "Centipede," and "Galaga." There's no air-conditioning and no bathrooms, but with "Mortal Combat" costing one token instead of the usual two, we weren't complaining. Be warned, though—on the "Space Shuttle" pinball machine, there are two slots to put in your token; choose the left one, the one that isn't lit. (The right one eats tokens, and the

Near the Electric Playground

attendant there is a real dick, so it was a hassle to get him to give us a refund.)

Another good thing about Electric Playground is that on Monday nights you get five tokens for a dollar instead of the usual four. We arrived on a Sunday but decided to spend the night so we could take advantage of this great

gaming deal. That gave us some extra time to go see the Grand Canyon, and we were going to, but *Porky's* was on TV again, and given the choice, there really was no choice. We went with *Porky's*.

Waiting for *Porky's*.

WRONG WAY **Travelers' Advisory**

How to Fix a Flat

It's bound to happen, folks! Especially when you're driving through Arizona on Highway 10. There's a good forty miles of nothing but shards of scrap metal, broken glass, and other antitire gadgets. It's a big joke out there in Arizona. They think it's *very* funny. Ruining a nice set of Michelins is a real goddamn hoot, apparently. I forgot how much of a laugh riot it really is! Definitely check it out. You'll laugh your ass off. Try to do it at high noon when it's so fucking hot you want to kill yourself. Yeah, it's great. Also, make sure you forget your wallet at the last motel so you have to end up blowing some gas station attendant for four shitty tires. Ask the sonofabitch for a Coke afterward. He won't give it to you. See if you can get some of the Polaroids he takes, too. Those'll be fun to look at later when you're down in the dumps. "Hey!" you'll say, "At least I'm not suckin' dick off Highway 10 to get a used set of Goodyears!" That'll make you feel better! The hell it will. You put a man's penis in your mouth for 150 pounds of steel-belted rubber, buddy, you won't be forgetting anytime soon. So deal with it. Now go change your own fucking tire. Make sure the damn car falls on your head and crushes your skull.

From the Phoenix Times

GORILLA & Co.   by Jill Bailey

Mr. James Peters, Anvil, Arizona

Few people know that Anvil, Arizona, is the home of the world's smuggest man. For seventeen years he has ignored reporters and refused to comment about his smugness. During the two weeks he spent in Anvil, he held two press conferences and merely drove by them slowly, grinning to himself.

He did attend the Continental Press Breakfast, but he sat by himself, reading Baudrillard and chuckling. He also wouldn't let us have any of the free Danishes because, he said, *we* couldn't truly appreciate them.

The Arizona Hall of Colons

No air-conditioning. No celebrities: colons. Dark. Hot. Damp. $18.50 for admission.

If you choose to enter the cave with professor Twangiri, turn to page 229.

If you choose to return to the boat with Panga, turn to page 250.

If you choose to go to Nevada, turn to the next page.

NEVADA

Nevada Gaming

Gambling and Nevada are inseparable in the country's consciousness. Let's face it. You just can't say "gambling" without saying "Nevada" in the same sentence. Okay, maybe that's a little bit of an exaggeration. I'm going to try to write a sentence using the word "gambling" without the word "Nevada" being in it as well. It's tough, though. The two sentences above have both had the words "gambling" and "Nevada" in them (as did this sentence). Okay, so it's difficult, but I'm going to give it a shot. Here we go. There is gambling. There, that's a sentence. Not a great sentence, but it will hold up in court. Sentence court if one existed. I have to admit, even though I didn't say "Nevada" in the sentence I created to prove a point, I did think it. So. Now. Where are we? Let's just say although it's possible to separate the word "gambling" from the word "Nevada" and put them in their own individual sentences, it's fairly difficult. Can we agree on that? I was only able to do it once on this whole page. And it certainly wasn't much of a sentence. There is gambling. I wouldn't be going out on a limb to say I won't be winning a Pulitzer for that particular sentence. I mean . . . maybe. If it's a slow year. Who knows. Crazier things have happened. If I got a phone call later this year and they told me I won a Pulitzer for the sentence "There is gambling," I'd be shocked. But I'd think in the back of my head, "Boy, you know everyone has a shot in this country. What a great country to live in. I'm so thankful I don't live in Turkey. I don't know the language. Wow, I won the Pulitzer. I have to call my mom."

Nevada**Attractions**

The Shumlertz Museum, Route 9, Nevada

A short drive east from Las Vegas is the most diverse and interesting art collection in this specific part of the United States. Housed in a bright orange, prefab structure (that's not as tacky as it sounds) is the Shumlertz Family Collection of lesser-known works by the great masters. You'll see:

Seurat's *Little Kid with Ringworm and No Eyes*
Manet's *Fat Lady Rubdown*
Van Gogh's *Self-Portrait of My Ass with a Raisin in It*
Renoir's *Balls!!*
Magritte's *Petit Enfant avec Ringworm et No Pas Oeilles*

And many more! Also, Bob Shumlertz's famous chili dogs.

Die Olde West Kampf, Surrogaut, Nevada

This treat for the whole family was a more traditional "Old West City" until it went bankrupt in '72 and was purchased by a commune of German Performance Artists.

You never know what to expect around the next corner, but you can sure count on one thing: It's probably going to become a godawful nightmarish product of a bleak twisted mind and would make even John Wayne shit in his pants.

It's always raining very old men from the ceiling of the saloon, the old-time barbershop is knee-deep in some sort of viscous brown-green gelatin (Tom seems to think it was very old mayonnaise; Kerri said creamed lentils), and a tape from the shop's basement repeats the word "hoffnugslos" endlessly.

The highlight of the town—the "High Noon Showdown"—lasts a grueling seventeen hours, during which the two gunslingers mash their own fingers with mallets. There's never a clear winner, but as Sheriff Staübig says: "Life is pain and death." While you're there, be sure to dine in Die Spindle Haus—the world's fastest-spinning bratwurst restaurant.

○ ○ ○ ○ *Las Vegas* ○ ○ ○ ○

Ahh—Las Vegas, city of contrast. Of culture and cuisine. Of medicine and magic. When one thinks of Las Vegas one usually thinks of the bright lights, the elaborate shows, and the decadent nightlife. What few people ever discover on a trip here is that Las Vegas is also home to a number of very fine casinos. They are not hard to find. When driving onto the Vegas Strip, simply stop by the Las Vegas Chamber of Commerce and ask the young vixen behind the desk for the addresses of some of the casinos in town.

Con Men, Cheats, and More

Be careful! Vegas is a lot of fun, but you could lose your savings faster than you can say "John Mellencamp" if you're not careful. Here are some common scams to watch out for:

The "Your Money or Your Life" Scam

This is the classic grift where the con man approaches you, the unsuspecting tourist, and puts a gun to your head, proclaiming that he'll shoot and kill you if you don't give him all your cash. This is a beautiful ruse because it puts you at the disadvantage: Your head could be blown off. Remember, if this guy was legit, he'd be getting his money some other way (job, inheritance, investment, etc.). Steer clear!

The "Faulty Headcase" Trick

We've all heard this one: You're at the blackjack table, and a stranger in a lab coat calls you over, complaining that his steel casing for his head isn't working properly. He seems legit because he's got this metal boxlike assembly that's just a little bigger than someone's head. You offer to test it by putting your head inside the pitch black, deadbolted, airtight chamber. It turns out there's nothing wrong with the casing, but in all the shuffle, you're out fifty bucks.

The "Free Rooms" Scam

An official-looking man asks if you and your spouse would like a free room, no strings attached. Naturally, you say yes. He shows you to the "free room." It's a nice, free hotel room, but there's no free lotion!

Beginners' Luck

If you've never gambled before, some people would suggest that the smartest thing to do would be to sit back and get familiar with the games, take some time to practice. It is obvious that these morons have never heard of a little thing called beginners' luck. Beginners' luck. Those two beautiful words are what protect you, the newcomer, from losing. Trust me.

So our advice to you is very simple, and we promise you this advice is the most valuable thing you will have to take away from this book.

If you have never gambled before and you don't understand the games, take out all the money you have in the bank and walk into that casino, head high, chest out, and bet, bet, bet.

Remember: You have beginners' luck on your side. And nobody, and we mean nobody, can take that away from you. Good luck. You'll have it! We guarantee you.

Whores

Also known as prostitutes, whores are a grand Las Vegas tradition. Some Dos and Don'ts:

DO: Ask for references: names of previous clients. You don't
      have to call them—just listen for famous names like Frank
      Sinatra or Judy Blume.

DO: Help whores zero in on your most erogenous zones by cir-
cling them with a thick black Magic Marker. Most whores can
lend you a marker for a modest ($1.50) charge.

DON'T: Be surprised if your whore has no heart of gold.

Getting Married in Las Vegas

So, for a goof, we all got married in Las Vegas, to each other. Which
we thought was going to be really funny, which it was . . . but the
problem is, I don't even want to be married to half the people in this
group. Not to mention that what we just did is completely illegal, so

From The Las Vegas Times

we're on the run from the law. Which could be seen as romantic, but with ten people it's not so romantic. There are so many cliques within the group that it's hard to spend good quality time with all of your spouses. So, we went to couples' therapy, which was very expensive. Everything is expensive when you're married to nine people. For instance, we went to Disneyland for our honeymoon, and it's eighty-five bucks a person! Now, I don't want to get into specific numbers, but eighty-five times ten is a lot. And that's not even counting the Mickey Mouse hats and the matching sweatshirts we bought. I'm feeling like maybe it's time we separated. I don't know, I guess my advice would be, if you're gonna get married on a whim in Vegas, try it out with one person first. And make sure they're not co-workers whom you're not the least bit attracted to or in love with.

Red Flag Hitchhikers

Nevada

CALIFORNIA

CALIFORNIA

Inside**Los Angeles**

While You're in Los Angeles, You May Want to Become a Movie Star

This is widely considered an almost insurmountable task, but we are about to give you INSIDE SHOW BUSINESS INFORMATION that will take you from pimpled-loserness to movie stardom in just a few simple steps. Remember, this is INSIDE SHOW BUSINESS INFORMATION intended only for you, the owner of this book, and not for your fat, pot-smoking friends.

Step 1: Go to the Creative Artist Agency (CAA) at 1750 Wilshire Boulevard and tell the receptionist that you'd like to sign up.

Step 2: Sign all the necessary paperwork. (You may want to bring a pen.) *Don't haggle over the 10 percent commission. It's standard showbiz b.s.*

Step 3: Give them your phone number and stress your interest in being involved only in feature projects that have a strong buzz and an A-list director attached.

Step 4: You're done! Congratulations, movie star. We'll see you at the big premiere!

A Word or Two about Rodeo Drive:
Things Not to Do in Chic Places

Don't go taking off your pants in no chic places

- Don't go taking off your pants in chic places. The type of folks who know how to groove on you taking off your pants don't go hanging out in no chic places.

- Don't go calling women "tramp" in no chic places even if you brought the women and know they can take a joke. Don't yell out, "You're a tramp" or "The women we brought are tramps." Places more lowbrow love this sort of thing, but *not* the folks in chic places.

- Don't crap yourself in chic places. It's frowned upon. If you must crap at a chic place, do it in an alley behind the kitchen (and don't go bragging about it).

- Don't go lighting farts in chic places—yours nor nobody else's. You won't get no cheers. They throw out folks who light farts in chic places.

- Don't go singing no songs about how you got crabs and banging pots around. Sure you think it's funny. I think it's funny, but they won't think it's funny in chic places.

- And finally, you ladies: Don't go shouting about your beaver in chic places. If the place is chic, then everyone has the good jobs and nice things to talk about and they don't want to go hearing about your beaver.

- Dress good and smell nice and don't go doing no stupid things and they won't throw you out of chic places.

A few of the differences we noticed between New York and L.A.: In L.A. you get plastic surgery; in N.Y. you get hit by a taxicab and need REAL SURGERY!!

In L.A. you drink mineral water; in N.Y. the water has plenty of minerals in it. RUST! (Yecch!!!)

In L.A. you worry about bad B.O. on opening weekend; in N.Y. you worry about bad B.O. on the subway. (Ewww!!)

L.A. has the Dodgers. In N.Y. everybody dodges TAXICABS! (Watch out!!!)

N.Y. has good bagels. In L.A. you can't find good bagels ANYWHERE! (*So* true!!)

L.A. has its "Hollywood" sign; N.Y.'s sign says "Homicide—Do not cross!!!" (Yikes!!!)

In N.Y. you get mugged in Times Square; in L.A. Jim Jay Bullock mugs on *Hollywood Squares*! (Huh?!?)

In L.A. Disney makes the ducks sing with the mice; in N.Y. Gotti makes the stool pigeons sleep with the fish! (And we don't mean ABE VIGODA!)

L.A. has its "Walk of Stars." If you walk in N.Y., muggers hit you with pipes and you SEE STARS! (**$#@!)

Every day in L.A. bright-eyed kids from Iowa get discovered; in N.Y. every day bright-eyed kids from Iowa get discovered naked, in Dumpsters near the West Side Highway with Coke bottles shoved up their ass!

Working in Los Angeles

Los Angeles is well known as a "tough town." In fact, Los Angeles, or L.A. as it's called by the people who live there, is home to America's largest porn industry. If you want to get into the porn business, you'll need to know exactly what to listen for. Porn directors can be very subtle, but if you want to get into porn, here are some normal-sounding lines that are actually veiled invitations to be in a porn movie.

b. "I'll bet you're great at porn."
c. "I'm not just saying this, but your dick is camera-ready."
d. "Like sex? How 'bout doin' it in a movie I'm making?"
e. "Those titties have porn written all over them."
f. "I'm going to film sexual intercourse up close. Interested?"
g. "I'd like to film you having sex with another person. A porno flick."
h. "I'm holding auditions for a porn movie next week. If you want to audition, you can rehearse the scene by having a lot of sex with someone."

([a] was not included for reasons beyond comprehension)

 Travelers' Advisory

When in Los Angeles, you will almost certainly be accosted by street physicians offering discount rhinoplasty. Many of these physicians are not licensed surgeons. It's better to wait and have your reconstructive surgery performed at the airport. (It's worth the extra thirty bucks in the long run.)

California**Activities**

Swim with the Accountants, Malibu, California

For a reasonable fee, you're fitted with a wet suit and lowered into a 20,000-gallon tank with five or six middle-aged accountants. As you enter their world, they playfully nudge you and just might invite you to join them in their game of Marco Polo. When you look into their large brown eyes it's almost like looking at a person who's not an accountant.

Marino relaxes after an invigorating swim with a tankful of CPAs

Shark cages are available but rarely necessary.

The *CANDID* Candid Camera Museum, Santa Monica, California

See the permanent exhibit that celebrates Allen Funt's short-lived risqué series on the Playboy Channel and home video. If you'll notice, the women who greet you as you enter the museum aren't exactly wearing tops. As you walk through, experience female security guards who, to your surprise, are not particularly dressed. As you leave, you'll be shocked to see several women who aren't quite as covered up as you might expect them to be. Smile!

California**Destinations**

Haight-Ashbury, San Francisco, California

When you think about Haight-Ashbury, you think about a couple of things. Hippies, marijuana pot, LSD, tie-dyed clothes . . . okay, maybe that's more than a couple of things, but we are stoned out of our minds. We have been in Haight-Ashbury for about three weeks now, and we are trippin'. So, here's what we're gonna do—here's what's easiest for us right now. We can't really complete our thoughts, so we're just gonna do a train of thought.

Okay . . . hippies really smell bad. My skin is very leathery right now, feel my jeans. Time is like . . . well . . . a lot like you. HA HA HA!!!! I'm NOT hungry but I could definitely eat something. You have pickles . . . don't even try it, buddy. You've got really beautiful pores. Pour me another, Jack. Jack? Beer tastes like water right now. Oh my oh my oh my oh my oh my oh my ohmaha, Neb. I Hate Ashberries!! HA HA HA!! WEEEEE! (sorry) Uh oh . . . okay. Not fun. Not fun anymore. I'm not sure where my shoes are. Kick this shit!!! FUCK YOU MOMMY! Ohhhhhhhhh . . . I got hankerin' fo' some cheese, please. Mr. See's. Ow! Let's lay down right here. Right here. Just look up. It's really cool. You see that tree? Mooo. MOOO. Moo Gooo Guy FLAN!?! I don't want to say this too loud, but I'm not a big fan of the Grateful Dead. Jerry Garcia Cherries!!! Where's Joe? JOE!!!!!!!!!!!!!!!!!! I feel like a poet. Who has the keys to the van? la la la la la la. I'm no Jerry.

Haight-Ashbury is located on the corner of Haight and Ashbury in the Haight-Ashbury District of San Francisco.

TRAVEL TIP

The San Diego Zoo

Sure, everyone loves a trip to the zoo (even cinemateur/screenwriter Roger Ebert), but there's no way to avoid the inevitable tension that accompanies these outings. It always happens, you're there at the zoo, it's a beautiful day, but nobody has a goddamn thing to say to each other. Next time this happens, why don't you lighten the mood a bit with a few aptly timed jokes? We recommend the following six jokes.

1. Hey, these monkeys remind me of your family.
2. Say, doesn't that monkey look like your sister?
3. (For parents) If you kids don't shut up, we're going to leave you here with your real family, the monkeys.
4. We should have asked to get in free since your sister is one of these monkeys.
5. There's no bureau mirror around, but in lieu of that, you can just look at a double of yourself in the monkey cage.
6. You know, if Leonard Nimoy did a "Search for Monkeys" show, he needn't come to this monkey cage; he might just as easily look in your home, at you and your sister.

Babaloo Mandel Birthplace, Outside of San Diego, California

Come join the pilgrimage and see the early roots of one of the most beloved co-writers in Hollywood. See the house that might have inspired *Parenthood* and visit the real city behind *City Slickers II*. The Mandel Museum includes the goofy Hawaiian shirt he wore while co-writing *Spies Like Us*, donuts he shared with Lowell Ganz as they were adapting *League of Their Own*, and this rare fax he received from Ganz in '85:

FAX

Fr: Lowell Ganz
To: Babaloo
Re: Summer Project

Baba Baby—

Opie called. Wants us to write a vehicle for Mike Keaton about Japanese folks making cars in the USA.

We need the work. I say lets do it.

Love, Low.

P.S. You still haven't been over to the new house. We're all gung-ho to have you and the wife for sodas and music videos. Say monday?

P.P.S. Start thinking about titles. Maybe "Keaton & The Japs"?

California**Activities**

Walk to Hawaii

During low tide you can walk across a sand dune in the Pacific Ocean from Long Beach, California, to any island in Hawaii. You'll be waist-high in salt water. Be sure to bring a six-pack and a snack; it's about a twenty-minute trek. Don't forget your swim trunks, neither! It's worth the effort.

A FEW WORDS ABOUT SAN BERNARDINO AND "DON'T TELL MAMA"

As you know, "Don't Tell Mama" is the second musical number in the Broadway hit *Cabaret*! This Kander and Ebb classic has been a staple in the American musical theater repertoire for over twenty-five years! But don't look for it in the major motion picture version of *Cabaret* starring Liza Minnelli; it got cut! "Don't Tell Mama" is not only a toe tapper, but it serves as an introduction to the character of Sally Bowles, the protagonist of *Cabaret*! In the song, Sally encourages the audience not to spill the beans to her mother that she's performing this risqué song! The lyrics are clever and the melody is memorable— that's what makes "Don't Tell Mama" a classic! In the movie version of *Cabaret* the order of the songs gets shifted around because "Don't Tell Mama" is not in it! (Not to mention "The Telephone Song"!) Even so, more people remember "Don't Tell Mama" than "The Telephone Song" because the lyrics are clever and the melody is memorable! Most people think of Liza Minnelli when they hear "Don't Tell Mama," but they're on the wrong track with that thinking! Liza Minnelli wasn't in the stage version of

fun fact

I'm sure we have all heard that San Francisco, California, is very hilly, but did you know that those hills were man-made? The original landscape of San Fran was as flat as my mom's ass. It only became hilly when the advertising executives over at Rice-a-Roni, Inc., thought it would be much more interesting to have the then very unpopular cable cars roaming a hilly terrain as opposed to a flat one in their now very popular commercial ad campaigns. It worked, boosting the stocks of Rice-a-Roni, cable cars, and, oddly enough, my mom's ass.

★

Cabaret; she was in the movie! And "Don't Tell Mama" wasn't! San Bernardino is in California.

A damp chill surrounds you as you find your way into the dark mouth of the cave. Professor Twangiri lights the lantern he purchased at the bazaar. With a sly smile he turns to you. "These were once catacombs, my young friend," he says. "I sense that we are closer now to the Ruby Lampeter than we have ever been, soon it can be returned to the parish at Tsambza, and you will have quite a story to tell."

As the professor turns, the flickering lamplight reveals the ancient skulls that line the narrow passageway. "We must find the bones marked with the Seal of Thebius," he whispers. "If Panga's map is correct, that is where Dr. Roche has hidden the . . . the . . ." Just then, a rumbling begins, as if a freight train were passing below the tomb. There is a warm rush against your ankles as the passageway fills with thick, warm . . . BLOOD! The blood rushes up to your knees as you struggle to retrace your steps to the mouth of the cave. The professor grasps for your sleeve as he slips, his piercing scream becomes gargles as his mouth fills with blood. In a flash, the lamp goes out! You feel your way along the bones to the entrance, only to find it sealed! The blood rushes up to your mouth and YOU ARE DEAD!

THE END

CHAPTER EIGHT

The Upper Left-Hand Corner

This area of the country is north of California, home of the Los Angeles Dodgers (and, needless to say, the San Diego Padres).

OREGON

OREGON

OREGON

If you are traveling to Oregon for the first time, there are a few things you need to know. Actually there's only one thing you need to know. Pot is legal in Oregon. Sure, that's great for the roadtrippin' college crowd, but for the rest of us, it can be a hassle. First of all, the only border marking is an enormous wall made of cheap basement paneling. There is one door with a handwritten notebook page that says "Oregon. Keep Out," held up by a bunch of radio-station bumper stickers. If you knock on the door, there will be no answer, even though you can clearly hear that a television is on and people are moving around, whispering. Keep knocking. A hairy Portuguese man named Ted will eventually open the door and promise to turn the TV down. Simply recite this phrase: "Yeah, uh . . . I'm a friend of Skeezer's?" and most likely Ted will let you in. If he refuses, and he tells you that Skeezer owes him money, just say: "Yeah, that sucks . . . I brought some beers." The door should swing wide. It is customary to hang out and watch cable with Ted and the rest of the population of Oregon for a few days, but if you're in a big hurry, just use this handy out: "Has anybody seen Chula?" Even though none of them knows anybody named Chula, they will tell you they "just saw him over there somewhere I think." Keep asking for Chula until you reach the next state, but for God's sake, if you find him, don't tell him we told where he was. We owe him money.

State Law You Should Know About

Oregon police will arrest anyone wearing a new pair of sneakers in public.

A Bit of History from Oregon

1968: Astronauts Buzz Aldrin and Neil Armstrong are the first men ever to step foot on the surface of Oregon's rocky terrain.

Oregon**Activities**

Chutney, Oregon

Chutney has a truly distinct niche among all the towns in this great nation of ours and it is this: The combined weight of the citizenry of Chutney is 183,505 pounds. This may not seem all that interesting until you couple it with the fact that only 245 people live in Chutney—meaning that the average weight of a Chutneyianer is a whopping 749 pounds, which is the ideal weight for an adult male if he's twenty-one feet tall, but sadly this is not the case. (The center for the Chutney Hoopsters, Antoine "Stretch" Mendoza, towers over his peers at five feet, two inches.)

When you arrive in Chutney, you'll find that self-esteem is always at low tide and that the spherical and sweaty locals have a penchant for hair pomade and menthol cigarettes. A general note: Try not to stare.

Start your tour of Chutney at the town square, where you'll probably find Mayor Freddy Goya bare-ass naked, passed out in a dry kiddie pool while his little tiny penis turns a pale pink in the midday sun. If you can wake him up, he'll probably cry and ask you for $5. You might want to stop for lunch at Rosie's Bottomless Cup o' Coffee (Franklin St.), where the coffee is served by the enormous and pantsless Rosie McNamara, who pushes herself to your table in a rusty wagon that smells like Indian food. If you look strong, Rosie will ask you to help with her ointment.

After lunch you'll probably want to hit the road so that you can avoid the "Sundown Moan and Roll," which is very, very awful.

A Guide to Coffee Shops in Portland

If you're in Portland, you'll no doubt find yourself in a coffee shop. If you don't know this already, coffee shops are a place for brooding, self-discovery, and intellectual debate. Coffee-shop mastery is a rare achievement, but here are some easy and impressive conversation possibilities for you.

- A reexploration of Derrida's term "Western Metaphysics," not only in the Western Philosophical Tradition but in "everyday" thought and language as well.
- The use of hyperreality as a means of deconstructing and exposing the intrinsic flaws and potentially catastrophic results of the Technology Age in *Blade Runner*.
- Gender Politics in Nineteenth-Century Europe: Work Identities for Men and Women in the Italian Dock Guilds, 1854–1860.
- The History of Male Victimization Paranoia in America: Discuss such topics as the Ku Klux Klan, Vigilantism, Militia Groups, and the Religious Right.
- Mythic Imagery and Stoicism in the works of Steinbeck, Fitzgerald, and Faulkner.
- Intellectual Perversion as it relates to the proliferation of increasing intangible paradigmatic methodologies.
- The Russian Experience: Explore the transformation of the Russian Empire—moving through the Czarist Era, the Bolshevik and Menshevik Revolutions, the rise and fall of Communism, ending with a discussion of new world possibilities as they affect a global economy and a new Russia in the age of Glasnost.
- Homer's *Iliad*; examine Hektor's *Darkened Heart*.

We hope these suggestions will be fun and useful as you experience the coffee shops of Portland, Oregon.

The Fantastic Fork-n-Spoon Festival, Joy, Oregon

It's a spoonerific extra-fork-gansa! You'll see spoons! Spoons! Spoons! and Forks! Forks! Forks! Forks! in this great celebration of two-thirds of our nation's everyday cutlery. Bring your whole family, your camera, and wear your "I'm-sure-ready-to-have-a-good-time-hat!" But be sure to leave your blade at home—they do pat you down at the door and are starting to employ metal detectors.

fun fact

Did you know? Every male resident of Eugene, Oregon, is named Thomas.

You see, back in '85 there was an argument between the United Spooners and the Fork Party over which eating utensil the baby Jesus used first. The row escalated into a fistfight, and unfortunately there were a lot of knives handy. (Back then it was an "All-Out Dining Utensils Festival.") Everyone was killed.

You can watch the whole fight on video at the Historical Society Tent, and every three years there's a reenactment. But as for me, I prefer the Spoonin' Jamboree, a Fork-n-Spoon Dog, and an Evening of Off-Color Fork Jokes at the Jeb Stuart Memorial Theater.

WASHINGTON

AREA CODE: (206)

BEST HAMBURGER: JUICY'S, Eugene

BEST GUY TO BUY POT FROM: Jarvis Turner, 206-232-9087

BEST GUY TO BUY ACID FROM: Leland Marsh, 206-344-0932

BEST GUY TO BUY SHROOMS FROM: Jarvis Turner, 206-232-9087

BEST GUY TO BUY "X" FROM: Jarvis Turner, 206-232-9087

BEST GUY TO BUY HASH FROM: Eddie McMarvel, 206-327-7432

BEST GUY TO BUY QUAALUDES FROM: Eddie McMarvel, 206-327-7432

BEST GUY TO BUY COKE AND METH FROM: Jarvis Turner, 206-232-9087

Let's face it, life's not worth it. Sure, we're all having a great time of it, yucking it up at the local five-and-dime now, but who knows what tomorrow will bring? Chances are nothing worth sticking around for. Hell, your wife is probably out right now fucking a farm animal. See what we mean?

We've got three words for you—"su" "i" "cide." (Or syllables, whatever. When you're dead nothing matters anymore.) And what better place to do the deed than in the rainiest, most depressing fucking city in the world—SEATTLE, Washington. Also home of the 1996 Western conference basketball champions, the SEATTLE SUPERSONICS!!! With Shawn Kemp! And Gary Payton! And the rest of the gang!!

So before you hook up that tube to your exhaust pipe, drive your car on over to the Key Arena and check out forty-eight minutes of some of the jamminest most crazy b-ballin' hoop shootin' slam dunkin' daddy-o's west of the Mississippi. Tickets range from $30 to $85. And the great thing about the Key Arena is . . . no seats are bad seats!!! Let's face it, you can take your life anytime, but how often do you get the chance to experience the SuperSonics battling some of the greatest teams in the world?

Like the Sonics vs. the Bulls! With Michael Jordan!! And Scottie Pippen!! Or, the Sonics vs. the Utah Jazz!! With Karl Malone!! And John Stockton!!

Or, the Sonics vs. the Los Angeles Lakers!! With Kareem Abdul-Jabbar!! And Jerry West!!!! Imagine the excitement of watching the Seattle SuperSonics playing basketball against the New York Knicks!! With Patrick Ewing!! And coach Jeff Van Gundy!!!

So, before you dive headfirst off the Space Needle, you should grab a *Seattle Times* and check the sports section for what kind of b-ball action is goin' down that night. Who knows? The Harlem Globetrotters may even be in town, and they're always a lot of fun!! With Curly!! And Happy Jackson!!! And Mr. Dribbles!!! And Mark!! And everybody's favorite . . . Downtown Bouncy Willis!!!! But don't be fooled, sometimes the bucket of water that they throw on you is really just little cut-up pieces of paper!!

So, you see, Seattle isn't just for suicide. It's for basketball, and good times. And there's also supposed to be a really neat fish market there somewhere. Check it out!

Seattle**Guide**

Seattle: Home of "Grunge"

Planning on washing your clothes en route to Seattle? Don't bother! The "Grunge" set won't accept you unless you don dirty clothes and an apathetic attitude. The most popular grunge band in Seattle is called Nirvana. Check local "zines" and "rags" for their next "gig."

When attending a "Grunge" concert, be understanding—most of these musicians are no Duke Ellington. But then again, you can't out-Duke the Duke. It can't be done. Don't be shocked to see performers dressed casually on stage. Blue jeans have taken over as the pant of choice for the younger generation. *(Continued on next page . . .)*

If a "gen X'er" strikes up a conversation with you, whatever you do, DON'T LABEL OR CATEGORIZE him/her. They hate that, and most of them keep sharpened screwdrivers hidden in their flannel shirts tied around their waists.

After the show, don't go back to the motel! Your "Grunge" night is not authentic without a visit to Starbucks for some coffee or Sanka.

Congratulations! You've now experienced the real Seattle—the one they never showed you in *Sleepless*.

The Old-Time Nike Shoe Cobbler, Seattle, Washington

Far off into the backhills of Washington lives an old, old cobbler who's been making shoes for Nike® for nigh onto fifty-seven years. He gets up at the crack of dawn, leaves his cottage, and drives all the way to Washington in his Lamborghini Hummer, where he pushes a button starting a machine that makes 200,000 shoes.

OVERHEARD AT THE LUMBERJACK, TACOMA, WASHINGTON:

GUY 1: That's Fred Beasley. He's a math teacher over at Tacoma Junior High. The kids love him, but the whole faculty despises him. He laughs like a sea lion, and all he eats is tuna fish.

GUY 2: That's pretty sad.

GUY 1: You should see his back.

GUY 2: What's with his back?

GUY 1: Got bumps all over it. Big, shiny bumps. Size of golf balls.

GUY 2: You've seen him naked?

GUY 1: We go to the same gym.

GUY 2: Gotcha.

Chapter Eight Comprehension Test

Chapter Four, The Interview

1. While she is in the prison cell, Master Brackett brings Hester Prynne a . . .
   a. Sandwich
   b. Bible
   c. Flower
   d. Physician

2. Hester Prynne and Roger Chillingworth are . . .
   a. Cousins
   b. Enemies
   c. Married
   d. Poor

3. Roger Chillingworth describes himself as . . .
   a. Handsome
   b. Unlucky but Rich
   c. Svelte
   d. Somber and Misshapen

4. Hester tries to hide this from Roger . . .
   a. The Baby
   b. A Knife
   c. The Scarlet Letter
   d. Herself

Suggested Activity

Try making your own scarlet letter with paper and a red felt-tip pen; OR use red paper. When you cut it out, it should look like this: A

CHAPTER NINE

Alaska
and Hawaii

T

hese two states are about as **opposite as you can get,** and yet they share one thing in common—we didn't go to either of them. As far as we can tell, Alaska is very cold most of the year, and the residents there eat nothing but whales. In Hawaii, they walk around naked, eat pineapples, and play basketball with volcanic rocks.

Both of these states came into the Union around the same time as a result of American imperialism, Manifest Destiny, the Monroe Doctrine, the New Deal, and Nixon's thing with China.

Both states have incredible things to see. For Hawaii, there are volcanoes, miles of beautiful beaches, and Don Ho. In Alaska, there are polar bears, glaciers, and local morning DJs. Also, the show *Northern Exposure* supposedly took place in Alaska, but not really. They shot the whole thing in, oddly enough, Hawaii. *Hawaii 5-0,* on the other hand, was shot in a remote village in Thailand. Nobody knows why.

Japanese people spend their vacations in Hawaii because

they can get clothes cheaper there than in Japan. As for Alaska, the Japanese rarely go there because Alaskans do not sell fashionable clothes.

Many people do not know that Hawaii is not one land mass but actually several islands connected by an intricate monorail system built in the time before Christ. These high-speed monorails float along an electromagnetic gravitational track that actually generates more energy than it consumes. Some historians say this "intercoastal monorail" rivals Stonehenge and the pyramids in terms of mystery.

Finally, sometimes it's funny to think about taking elements from Hawaii and putting them in Alaska, or vice versa. For example, a polar bear surfing. That's pretty funny.

ALASKA

Okay, nobody told us that in Alaska nights are six months long. We guess we should have known, but we didn't, and it really screwed up our sleeping patterns. For example, we usually wake up like one or maybe two times a night to go to the bathroom. We got up literally 3,742 times. That's a lot of times.

JOE'S SKETCHBOOK —

ALASKA'S HOWARDS!

HOWARD DELASSIS
PET SHOP OWNER

HOWARD GUSHUE
MOVIE USHER

HOWARD MACKEY
MATH TEACHER

Dungeons and Dragons

Alaskans take their D&D very seriously. No one is permitted to enter the state without rolling a 7, 16, or a 3. Elves and Charmers of Gelfin are exempt ONLY if they have an Invisible Cloak.

HAWAII

A Bit of History from Hawaii

On Tuesday, November 11, at 5:49 P.M., the Hawaii Insurrection for Freedom from America began. At 6:30 P.M. (just in time for *Jeopardy*), the Insurrection threw in the white flag and reclaimed its loyalty to the States. No one was injured. No one even knew it had happened.

State Law You Should Know About

Going abroad and coming back to America with 'tude is a Section 8 Felony under Penal Code 5.

HawaiiAttractions

While not a particularly unique state, Hawaii does have its share of attractions. Most notably is the Starbucks in the downtown Honolulu commercial plaza. Try the Frappuccino—it's delicious. Other Hawaii highlights include the Starbucks Mocha Frappuccino and the Mocha Java.

You wave good-bye to the professor as he disappears into the dark passageway. "The professor, he will die in there," says Panga. "Quickly, to the boat—it's almost cocktail hour!" Within moments, the mules have you back on board the *Marguerite*. "What took you so long," asks Emile with a wink. "I've finished the banana coladas, and Veronique and the twins are waiting below for you to powder their naked asses." You slip out of your dusty boots to enjoy the new shag carpeting on the deck and watch as the sun sets over the new go-cart/paintball/casino on the mainland. All the while, the strains of Grand Funk Railroad waft through the summer air. "And by the way," adds Emile in a low whisper, "I've filled the tub with penne."

THE END

CHAPTER TEN

Road
Games

Everybody enjoys spending hundreds of hours in a cramped automobile, but sometimes even the most interesting journeys can get a tad tedious. Which is why we've compiled a list of some of our favorite road games that everybody can enjoy. Most road games tend to give the more intelligent people in the car an unfair advantage, just because they're smart, but these are games everybody can enjoy— even total retards!

Road Game #1
TWENTY

Twenty is a terrific road game in which skill and intelligence take a "back seat" to teamwork and perseverance. We'll "count" you in!

Requirements: Two to six players, referee (with enclosed scorecard), and car lighter.

Object: To get from one to twenty, back to one, back to twenty, and so on.

How to play Twenty: Referee begins the game by selecting a player to start. The first player begins by saying the first whole number, one. The player sitting counterclockwise to the first player then says the next whole number, two. Play continues with each player in turn counting by ones until the total reaches twenty, at which time all the players shout, "TWENTY!" and clap hands. The direction of play then reverses, so the player sitting clockwise from the player who reached "Twenty" begins counting backward, until the counting returns to one, at which time all players pretend to cry like eensy-weensy babies and go, "Wah! Wah! Wah!" Then the counting begins anew!

The referee uses the scorecard to determine whether or not the counting is correct. If any player says the wrong number, or speaks out of turn, he or she gets a "strike." After three strikes, a player sits out one turn and then rejoins the game with zero strikes. The game is over when all players mutually decide to end. If some players decide to stop but others wish to keep playing, the game can and must continue.

Any disputes are referred to the referee. The referee's decision in all disputes is final, unless a majority of players vote to override the referee's decision, in which case the referee's call is reversed and the referee is given a "strike." If the referee receives three strikes, the strongest player uses the car lighter to burn the referee.

Road Game #2
BEGINNERS' ROAD BINGO

Road Bingo is an endlessly fascinating way to pass the time during a long car trip. It's played just like regulation Bingo, except instead of crossing off numbers, the player crosses off things he (or she!!!) finds "on the road." This version is designed for the beginner, but we think players of all levels will enjoy spying these stumpers! And just like in regulation Bingo, the winner gets a bare-bottom paddling. Yummy!

B	I	N	G	O
Seat Belt	Roof	Finger	Outside	Any Kind of Writng
FREE SQUARE	Steering Wheel	Clothes	Road Bingo Board	Freckle
Person	Person	FREE SQUARE	Person	Person
Yourself	Inside	The Road	Dome Light	Player's Choice
Something	Car	Soft Thing	Karl Malden	FREE SQUARE

Road Game #3
WHAT DID I HAVE FOR LUNCH?

If you're hungry for a great guessing game, have we got a treat for you! What Did I Have for Lunch? combines the delicate flavor of Concentration, the zest of a Sherlock Holmes mystery, and just a hint of high-stakes, Las Vegas–style poker. Bon Appetit!

Requirements: Three to five players, one player to be "It," thirteen
  twenty-sided dice (available at most hobby shops), a stopwatch.
Object: To guess what "It" ate for lunch.
How to play What Did I Have for Lunch?: At the start of the game,
  the players determine who will be "It." To do this, all thirteen
  twenty-sided dice are thrown. The total of the dice is added.
  Whoever's total is closest to 260 is "It" for the first round. Play
  begins when "It" asks the question, "What did I have for lunch?"
  and starts the stopwatch. All players begin simultaneously
  shouting out guesses. The round ends when one player success-
  fully guesses what "It" had for lunch. Following is a sample
  round:

> **"It":** What did I have for lunch?
> **Player 1:** Hamburger?
> **"It":** No.
> **Player 2:** Cheeseburger?
> **"It":** No.
> **Player 3:** Cold cuts?
> **"It":** No.
> **Player 2:** A taco?
> **"It":** No.
> **Player 1:** Grilled cheese?
> **"It":** No.
> **Player 3:** Pizza?
> **"It":** Yes.

(Everybody claps and congratulates Player 3. Some congratula-
tory remarks might be: "Good guess," "Terrific guess," "Fine

guess," "I liked your guess," "Great guess," "What religion are you?" etc.)

When the correct answer is gotten, the player who guessed correctly becomes "It" and play resumes. If nobody guesses the correct answer within three minutes, the car is sped up and driven into a tree. The game is over when all players have been "It," or the car is driven into a tree.

Some hints for players: Don't waste time on clever guesses like "Trout," because that only wastes precious time. Stick with common lunchtime items, and if you already know what "It" had for lunch, that's a real advantage.

Road Game #4
LICK THE SEAT BELTS

Here's a great game that's exciting, fun, and a fabulous opportunity for players to use their mouths in a whole new way—namely, by licking the seat belts!

Requirements: One to six players, seat belts, a car radio with a digital clock, handi wipes, thirteen twenty-sided dice (available at most hobby shops).

Object: To lick those seat belts!

How to play Lick the Seat Belts: Players roll thirteen twenty-sided dice. Whoever's total is closest to 260 checks the car radio's digital clock and screams, "PUT OUT THE SEAT BELT FIRE!!!" Simultaneously, all players begin licking their seat belts. Seat belts may be worn or not worn, but players can and must lick all parts of the seat belt, including the strap. Players may not lick another player's seat belt. Players should be careful to lick both sides of the seat belt. The game is over when five hours have elapsed.

One rule: Once play begins, players may not stop licking their seat belts for any reason. At the end of the game, players put the handi wipes in their eyes, and sing a round of "Thumby, the Dirty Shoemaker."

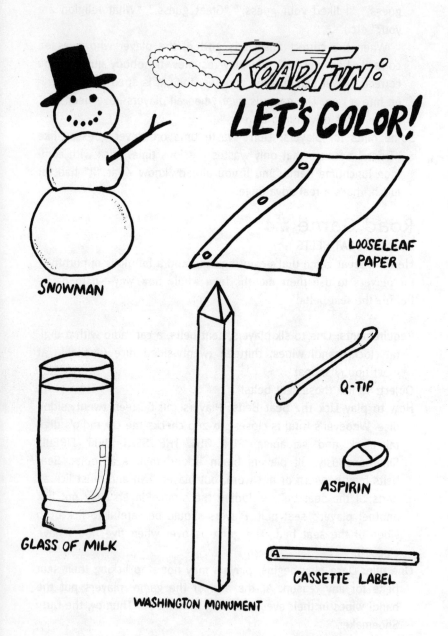

SNOWMAN

LOOSELEAF PAPER

GLASS OF MILK

WASHINGTON MONUMENT

Q-TIP

ASPIRIN

CASSETTE LABEL

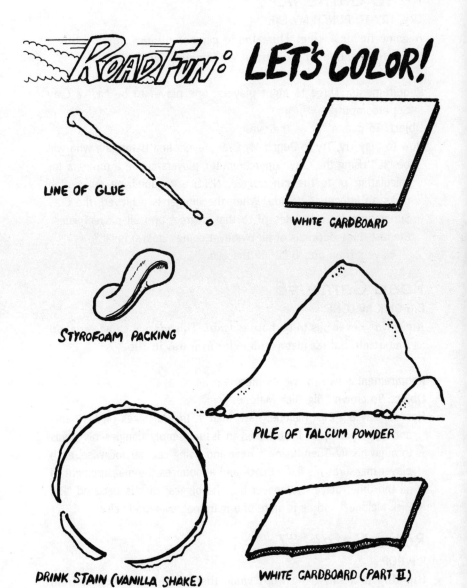

RoadFun° LET'S COLOR!

LINE OF GLUE

WHITE CARDBOARD

STYROFOAM PACKING

PILE OF TALCUM POWDER

DRINK STAIN (VANILLA SHAKE)

WHITE CARDBOARD (PART II)

Road Game #5
TRY, TRY TO PUNCH MY EYE

A game fit for a king! This simple game combines quick reflexes and determination for the ultimate in traveling fun.

Requirements: Three to eight players, one player to be "It," a Cray Supercomputer.

Object: To punch "It" in the eye.

How to play Try, Try to Punch My Eye: Players first determine who will be "It." Using the Cray Supercomputer, players create a program for calculating pi to the nth degree. Next, a randomizing subroutine picks an integer $\geq$ 10,000. When the integer is achieved, the Cray Supercomputer calculates pi to that degree, and all players guess the last three decimals of pi. Whoever comes closest is "It."

Players then punch "It" in the eye.

Road Game #6
BIG DICK MALONE

A car ride never has to be boring again. This classic game is as old as time itself, but it's just as fun today as it was in 1962.

Requirements: Two to twenty men, a ruler.

Object: To crown "Big Dick Malone."

How to play Big Dick Malone: Each man in the car takes off his pants and underpants, or if space is an issue, simply dangles his penis through his fly. Then, using a ruler and going counterclockwise, each player measures his flaccid cock and announces the measurement to all the other players. Whoever has the biggest dick is declared "Big Dick Malone," and he is more of a man than everybody else.

Road Game #7
RIP ROP

Rip Rop is a satisfying word game that will elicit chuckles from admirers but can be very annoying. Like all great games (Chess, Mastermind, Boggle), the premise of the game is simple, but the subtleties can take a lifetime to master. Here's how to play:

Someone in the car says a word in the normal course of conversation. Then you take the word that person said, add "Rip Rop" before it, and put the "R" at the head of the word itself. Some examples:

> **Your friend:** I hope this road isn't too dangerous.
> **You:** Rip Rop Rangerous.
> **Your friend:** We should check out Hoover Dam.
> **You:** Rip Rop Roover Ram.

A great game because you can start playing it without the consent of your fellow travelers. Sometimes "Rip Rop" is not as appropriate for the situation as other variations; for example:

> **Your friend:** By the end of the day we'll be in Colorado.
> **You:** Slip Slop Slolorado.
> **Your friend:** What's tonight's schedule?
> **You:** Krip Krop Kredule?

The possibilities are limitless. The true art of this game, of course, is to know instinctively which words deserve what treatment, and which words should be left alone. Grandmasters of Rip Rop play this game (if sometimes under their breath) twenty-four hours a day. Good Luck!

As you can tell, there is no end to the variety of games one can play during a long road trip, and we hope this small sample will keep fun in the "driver's seat" for a long time to come!

Road Game #8
KICK THE CAR

Now this is a game for all ages (with the exception of sixty-three-year-olds). And you can play it while you're driving or at any rest stop across the country. The rules are simple: Kick the car—as soft or as hard as you would like; we suggest a medium-strength kick. That way you will see results but not harm your toes from stubs. What's great about this game is that there are no losers. Everybody wins.

Equipment: 1 car
Legs

Road Game #9
ADVANCED BEGINNERS' ROAD BINGO

For the player who has mastered Beginners' Road Bingo! This version is a little more challenging, but just as fun. Good luck!

B	I	N	G	O
French Provisional Government	Reality	Catholic Diocese	Stop Sign	Painting by Jean Michel Basquiat
Lungfish	Barn	Nano-genarian	Heir Apparent	Chinook
School	Surrogate Mother	**FREE SQUARE**	Loggins and Messina	Theocrat
Dungeon Master	π	Hoffa	Retired Circus Elephant	Billboard
Handwritten Apology from Leon Trotsky	Fire Truck	Largess	Karl Malden	Grass-Roots Coalition

Road Game #10
SPIT IN THE CAR

Talk about passing time the fun way. This game will keep you spitting for hours. If that's what you want to do. Here are the rules: Spit in the car. Anywhere. On the window, on the other window, or on your lap. It doesn't matter as long as you spit, and if the car slows down so a deer can cross the street, don't let that distract you—keep spitting or you LOSE.

Equipment: 1 car
An abundance of saliva

Road Game #11
SHIT! (THE VERB) OR SHIT IN THE CAR
This one's great.

All you have to do is shit in the car. Whoever shits wins.

Tip: It helps to be regular.

Road Game #12
THE MILE-MARKER GAME
Here's a fun way to pass the time when you're driving along the lonesome highway.

PLAYER ONE pretends that he or she is famous radio personality Ruth Babbish, and he or she will be introducing the world-renowned mile-marker reader Jim Stansel. PLAYER TWO pretends to be Stansel. Here's an example game:

    Player 1: "Good afternoon, ladies and gentlemen, and thank you all for joining us. We're here on Interstate Route 80, heading west toward Ohio, and we are lucky enough to be joined today by Jim Stansel, the standard setter for mile-marker readers the world over. Jim has just returned from a European tour, where he read mile markers in Venice, Scotland, and Brubeck. And now he'll be reading for us here today. I think the next one is coming up now. Ladies and gentlemen, I give you the one, the only, the incomparable Jim Stansel!"

    Player 2: *(pretending to be Stansel)* "481."

Travel Songs
"HAPPY BIRTHDAY"

Tip: "Happy Birthday" is a great song to sing on the road. It's happy (one need not look further than the song's title), and its subject matter is a uniquely American institution: The Birthday. What few of us realize, however, is that it *is* possible to sing "Happy Birthday" on a road trip even if there is no one celebrating a birthday that day. Just make the following adjustment to the familiar lyrics:

Conventional Lyric:

> Happy birthday to you.
> Happy birthday to you.
> Happy birthday dear (INSERT NAME HERE [e.g., "Wilgreen"]).
> Happy birthday to you.

New Lyric for Car Trips with No Birthday Celebrators Present:

> Happy birthday to you.
> Happy birthday to you.
> Happy birthday dear "SO AND SO."
> Happy birthday to you.

"THUMBY, THE DIRTY SHOEMAKER"

> On streets of gold, in times of old
> Lived Thumby, the dirty shoemaker.
> Children were told to cross the road when they saw
> Thumby, the dirty shoemaker.
>
> His teeth were coal. His face was mold.
> Thumby, the dirty shoemaker.
> His hair was toads. In his pants, the load
> Of Thumby, the dirty shoemaker.
>
> But one thing was clean, and that was Thumby's dream
> To be the town's filthiest shoemaker.
> But there was a clause in the town's laws
> Which recognized Garret as the town's filthiest shoemaker
> Even though Garret wasn't very dirty at all,
> But his father was friends with the mayor.
>
> Oooooh, Thumby, the dirty shoemaker.
> Thumby, the dirty shoemaker.
> Thumby, the dirty shoemaker.
> Thumby, the dirty shoemaker.
> Thumby, the dirty shoemaker.
> Thumby, the dirty shoemaker.
> Thumby, the dirty shoemaker.

Thumby, the dirty shoemaker.
Thumby, the dirty shoemaker.
Thumby, the dirty shoemaker.
Thumby, the dirty shoemaker.
Oooooh Thumby, the dirty shoemaker.
Thumby, the dirty shoemaker.
Thumby, the dirty shoemaker.
Thumby, the dirty shoemaker.
Thumby, the dirty shoemaker.
Thumby, the dirty shoemaker.
Thumby, the dirty shoemaker.
Thumby, the dirty shoemaker.
Thumby, the dirty shoemaker.
Thumby, the dirty shoemaker.
Thumby, the dirty shoemaker.
Thumby, the dirty shoemaker.
Thumby, the dirty shoemaker.
Thumby, the dirty shoemaker.
Thumby, the dirty shoemaker.
Thumby, the dirty shoemaker.
Thumby, the dirty shoemaker.
Thumby, the dirty shoemaker.
Thumby, the dirty shoemaker.
Thumby, the dirty shoemaker.
Thumby, the dirty shoemaker.
Thumby, the dirty shoemaker.
Thumby, the dirty shoemaker.
Thumby, the dirty shoemaker.
Thumby, the dirty shoemaker.
Thumby, the dirty shoemaker.
Thumby, the dirty shoemaker.
Thumby, the dirty shoemaker.
Thumby, the dirty shoemaker.
Thumby, the dirty shoemaker.
Thumby, the dirty shoemaker.

Happy Trails!

INDEX